TWIN KILLERS

Dispatches Against
Global Apartheid
& Planetary Ecocide

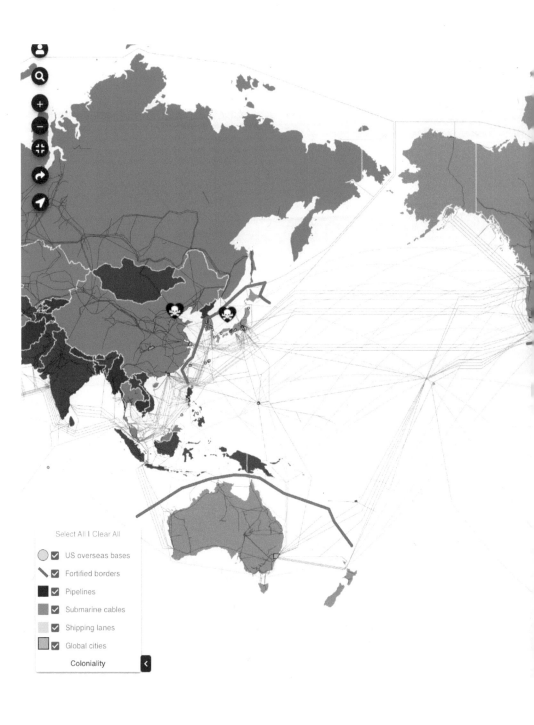

Select All | Clear All

- ☑ US overseas bases
- ☑ Fortified borders
- ☑ Pipelines
- ☑ Submarine cables
- ☑ Shipping lanes
- ☑ Global cities

Coloniality ‹

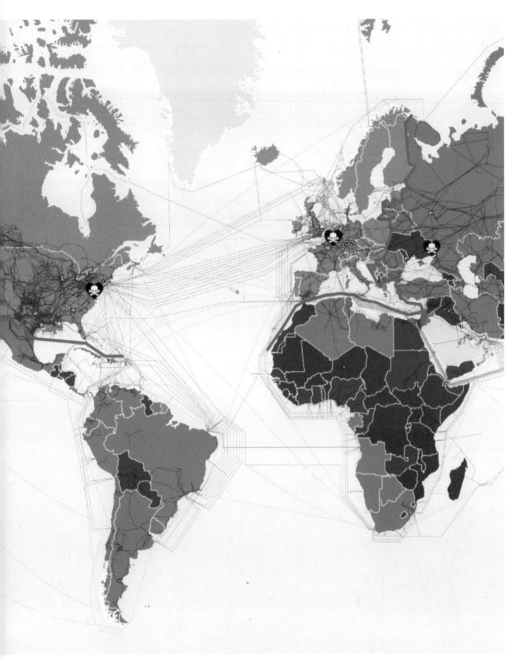

Mapping the logistics of Racial Capitalist Empire. From TwinKillers.org

SFPML

www.solutionsforpostmodernliving.org

First Printing, 2023

Copyright © 2023 by Muindi Fanuel Muindi

Designed by Muindi Fanuel Muindi

ISBN 979-8-218-22520-9

Kwa bibi zangu
For my grandmothers

CONTENTS

Author's Note

This book only features my name on its cover but it was written in response to, in collaboration with, and with encouragement from family, friends, and fellow travelers.

Deserving of full credit for the finest features of the work but no admonishments for the work's faults, which I assume — I name them here as my co-authors:

Ylfa Muindi, Nyamisi Muindi, Quincēy Xavier, Colin Stragar-Rice, Alisha Sharma, Sarah Bitamazire, Whitney Paul, Jordan Stanford, Jak'Quan Jackson, Alexandria Brantley, Sophie Daws, and Greg Saunier.

I owe very special thanks to Greg Saunier, whose comments and edits to the final drafts of this book were invaluable to me, not to mention his friendship and enthusiasm.

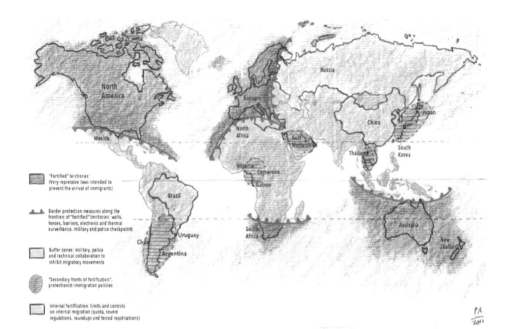

"Fortified" territories:
(Very repressive laws intended to prevent the arrival of immigrants)

Border protection measures along the frontiers of "fortified" territories: walls, fences, barriers, electronic and thermal surveillance, military and police checkpoints

Buffer zones: military, police and technical collaboration to inhibit migratory movements

"Secondary fronts of fortification": protectionist immigration policies

Internal fortification: limits and controls on internal migration (quota, severe regulations, roundups and forced repatriations)

INTRODUCTION

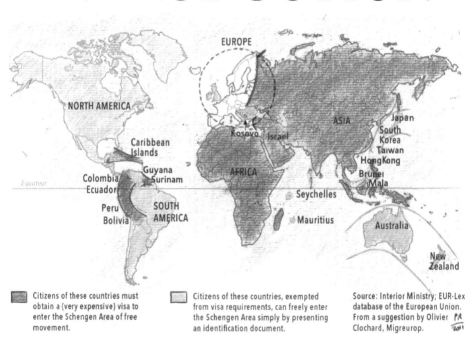

Citizens of these countries must obtain a (very expensive) visa to enter the Schengen Area of free movement.

Citizens of these countries, exempted from visa requirements, can freely enter the Schengen Area simply by presenting an identification document.

Source: Interior Ministry; EUR-Lex database of the European Union. From a suggestion by Olivier Clochard, Migreurop.

It reads like the set up for a Hollywood science fiction but it is, in fact, our world today:

Life on our beautiful blue-green planet is being depleted and devastated by a global apartheid regime engineered by a Racial Capitalist Empire bent on planetary ecocide.

As our story begins, a hundred million human beings are already displaced; 2 billion are hungry and 4 billion in poverty; climate catastrophes have only just begun and are likely to submit hundreds of millions more, if not a billion, to these same plights; the planet's wildlife populations are experiencing a precipitous decline, having plummeted more than two-thirds over the past 50 years; half of the planet's languages are in danger of extinction and likely to disappear within the next century; and the social and economic fallout from a global pandemic has inspired the governments of the whiter, richer nations at Empire's core to blow their bureaucratic, militarized border regimes out of all proportion, to repulse peoples from the darker, poorer nations of the periphery.

The powers and privileges that have yielded such psychopathic cruelties are reserved for "white men" who preach the "gospel of growth" and for that "talented tenth" that aids and abets them as proxies and redeemers — the latter having been fractioned off from demographic groups otherwise subject to dispossession, denigration, exploitation, and extermination.

To make matters even worse, the Empire's floundering hegemon is using its "discretion" to fund its police and military forces above all else in preparation for who knows what...

Hollywood and its many imitators have imagined ecological collapse, pandemics, and the rise and fall of a dystopian Empire bent on destroying all life on Earth, but they have imagined it all as fast-paced, linear, hypnotic excitement, with events unfolding in accelerating succession like the downing of cleverly placed rows of dominoes. In reality, it has been a deathly, nebulous, 600 year slog.

The Hollywood imagination has warped our sense of reality to such an extreme that many of us struggle to grasp the events of immense import that are now unfolding — slowly, surreptitiously, and in a non-linear fashion. What's more, the Hollywood imagination, with its councils of ingenious and self-consciously venal elites and caricatures of villainous conspiracies, blinds us to the less spectacular but more disturbing reality: the opportunistic collusion of unconscious ethno-class interests that has quietly maintained and advanced global apartheid, and derived both pleasure and profit from perpetrating and perpetuating planetary ecocide. In so doing, the Hollywood imagination has also effectively eroded our ability to even recognize movements of peoples endeavoring to overthrow global apartheid and put a stop to planetary ecocide.

The Arthouse imagination, positing itself as the alternative, turns out to play its own role in this erosion. As learned academics and aesthetes dazzle us with so many inventions and subversions of formal conventions, they prevent us from attending to their indifference to disturbing content and oppressive contexts. The Arthouse imagination does for the refined taste what the Hollywood imagination does for the crude masses: fool us into thinking that our everyday lives are boring, ugly, and meaningless compared to the fantasies that they each serve us as diversions. Different means towards the same end, they both make it easier to imagine a catastrophic end of everything, and more difficult to imagine a graceful end to the global apartheid that is pushing planetary ecocide.

My aim in writing and publishing this book is to counter the debilitating effects of the Hollywood and Arthouse imaginations, and to enable my readers not only to imagine but, better still, to recognize past and present radical peoples' movements against the twin killers of global apartheid and planetary ecocide.

Reading this book, some will discover that, unbeknownst to themselves, they have already been participating in radical peoples' movements in the most unexpected of ways. Others will discover that they have unwittingly been complicit in the crushing of radical peoples' movements. And a good many will discover that they have been, by bizarre twists of fate and circumstance, either by turns, or at one and the very same time, both vital supporters of and fatal accomplices to the destruction of these movements. Consciously or unconsciously, we are all playing a part in the most epic battle for the life and beauty of the Earth: the struggle between the wild and rebellious forces of Nature, and the genocidal, ethnocidal, and ecocidal forces of Empire. Ay, and the imperative for those who discover themselves on the wrong side of this conflict is to make every effort to desert the forces of Empire, and defect to the forces of Nature.

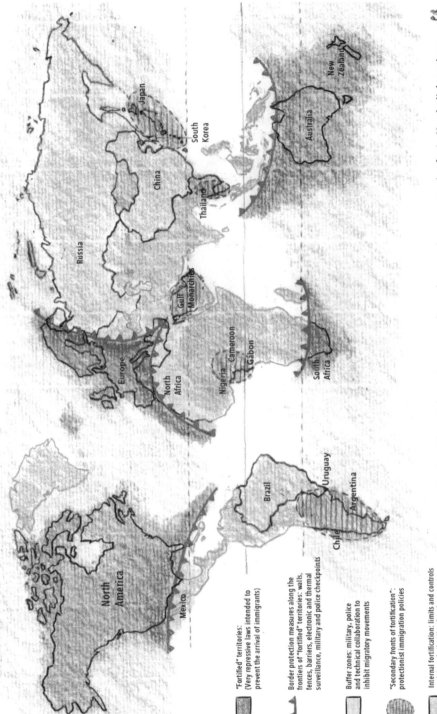

"Fortified" territories:
(Very repressive laws intended to prevent the arrival of immigrants)

Border protection measures along the frontiers of "fortified" territories: walls, fences, barriers, electronic and thermal surveillance, military and police checkpoints

Buffer zones: military, police and technical collaboration to inhibit migratory movements

"Secondary fronts of fortification": protectionist immigration policies

Internal fortification: limits and controls on internal migration (quota, severe regulations, roundups and forced repatriations)

Map by Philippe Rekacewicz, a journalist and geographer, cartographer for Le Monde diplomatique

TEK
& THE TECHNO-SPHERE

It would have made sense, before being thrown into today's deathly world of suffering, and being forced to make agonizing ethical choices within it, for us all to have been given some minimal backstory and context — a map to help orient us with respect to the twin scourges, global apartheid and planetary eco-cide, that will confront us during our time amongst the living here on Earth.

Sadly, most of us haven't. But, I say, better late than never…

Imagine, if you will, the next episode of your life as a film. What follows is the film's opening crawl, situating your life within the natural history of your species, Homo sapiens…

For tens of thousands of millennia, most humans have lived in immense and complex societies together with great multitudes of non-human others. Humans and non-humans had comparable influence within these social poly-cultures. Indeed, for most of human history, humans and non-humans have been so intimately and deeply involved in each other's lives that, more often than not, humans have regarded and treated all non-human others — animal, vegetal, and elemental — with the same deference as they have other humans.

It was commonplace for humans to regard the winds, the rains, the seas, the soils, the rocks, the clouds, the sun, and the moon as peoples; to regard the trees, the shrubs, the herbs, the grasses, the mosses, the lichens, and the fungi as peoples; to regard the birds, the insects, the fish, the reptiles, the amphibians, and all our fellow mammals as peoples.

Today, such commonplaces are too often haughtily dismissed as superstitious "primitivisms," and those humans who adhere to such commonplaces dispossessed, dehumanized, denigrated, and dismissed from consideration, as "primitives."

Why and how has this come to pass?

500 years ago, a dramatic social shift took place. Some groups of humans increasingly began to distinguish themselves from and claim dominion over non-human others and to organize themselves into "human, all too human" societies, social monocultures in which humans are far and away the most influ-ential social actors. What's more, some humans increasingly began to distinguish themselves from and claim dominion over other humans, casting these others as dehumanized "races," and treating them as derisively and dismissively as they did non-human others.

What happened 500 years ago was not entirely unheard of. The first highly "successful" and expansionary "human, all too human" social arrangements achieved great prominence and then died out millennia ago — these being the patriarchal and imperial "military-slavery-coinage complexes" of the Axial

Age empires (800 BC - 600 AD). Other such social arrangements have periodically re-emerged and died out ever since. The uniqueness of the dramatic social shift that took place 500 years ago had less to do with the emergence of "human, all too human" social arrangements per se, and more to do with their extreme virulence and violence. Turbo-charged by a fusion of racist and capitalist techniques and technologies of power, these were the imperialist white-supremacist capitalist patriarchies of the Euro-Atlantic West.

The practice of distinguishing oneself as human and claiming dominion over both non-human others and dehumanized humans has come to be called "human civilization," and the human groupings who practice it have come to be called "civilized peoples." The extreme virulence and violence of the "human, all too human" social arrangements that emerged and spread from the Euro-Atlantic West to the rest of the world have yielded a human civilization so "advanced," and peoples so "civilized," that they have come to define a new ecocidal geological era that is, itself, "human, all too human": the Anthropocene.

This era is characterized by the emergence of a new Earth sphere: the technosphere. Once, everything in Earth's system could be placed into one of four interlocking natural subsystems: the lithosphere (landforms), hydrosphere (water), biosphere (lifeforms), and atmosphere (air). The technosphere is a new, artificial subsystem made up of the assembled technologies and infrastructures of the "human, all too human" lifeways that emerged and spread from out of the Euro-Atlantic West. The ecocidal horrors of the Anthropocene are attributable to the harmful effects of the rapid growth and spread of this technosphere on the natural regeneration and renewal of the atmosphere, biosphere, hydrosphere, and lithosphere.

Prior to the Anthropocene, to the extent that the greater part of humanity lived in more-than-human societies in which non-human others were influential social actors, Transformative Ecological Knowledges (TEK) prevailed over and against "human, all too human" technologies and infrastructures. TEK was integral to the natural regeneration and renewal of the atmosphere, biosphere, hydrosphere, and lithosphere. The repression and ruination of TEK, everywhere and anywhere it was inconveniently found, enabled the rapid emergence and growth of the "human, all too human" technosphere, and brought about the Anthropocene.

The advance of "human, all too human" civilization and the repression and ruination of TEK have benefited a minority of human beings, primarily those peoples belonging to the so-called "white" race and those "non -white" peoples who serve the peoples of the white race as proxies and redeemers. Otherwise, the vast majority of non-human others and the dispossessed and denigrated races of humanity have suffered and endured ruin.

Over that past five centuries, hundreds of millions, if not more than a billion dehumanized humans have been tortured and murdered by the civilized peoples of the Euro-Atlantic West and their proxies and redeemers. We shall tend to these tortured and murdered multitudes later in this book. For now, let us simply recognize that the past sufferings of tortured and murdered multitudes are inextricable from present sufferings. And things only seem bound to get worse. Rampant fossil fuel consumption, driven by the growth and spread of the "human, all too human" technosphere, is transforming the atmosphere of the Earth. A phase change from a relatively stable climate to a chaotic climate is currently underway. Climate chaos will decimate wildlife habitats and cause more frequent and fierce droughts, floods, and famines. The results of all this being (i) that wildlife populations will not only drop further but faster, (ii) that hundreds of millions, if not billions more humans will endure hunger and poverty, and (iii) that cultures and languages rooted in landscapes that have been rendered unlivable by droughts, floods, and famines will themselves be driven to extinction.

In order to survive this ongoing planetary ecocide, the vast majority, inclusive of both the dehumanized races of humanity and non-human others, must band together to (i) deconstruct and desert the "human, all too human" civilizations that are currently prevailing over the planet and furthering planetary ecocide, (ii) recover and gather together the remnants of ancestral TEK that have managed to survive the advance of "human, all too human" civilizations, and (iii) (re-)construct ancestral TEK and (re-)create more-than-human societies anew, complementing them so that they are better able to confront the challenges wrought by the Anthropocene.

Survival will not be an easy feat. The "human, all too human" civilizations prevailing over the planet today are ruthlessly committed not only to protecting their existing powers and privileges, but to advancing them. They are presently promoting "solutions" to the challenges of the Anthropocene that involve extending the reach and intensifying the grip of their technosphere over the planet. They have engineered a global apartheid regime that serves to keep the dispossessed and denigrated races under their domination and control, and ripe for exploitation. The planners and technocrats who administer and supervise the advance of civilization are telling us that geo-engineering projects, carbon capture services, and renewable technologies made from vast quantities of rare earth metals extracted from the lands of the denigrated races of humanity, will ensure "sustainability" from here on out. What this means, in reality, is the "managed depletion" of the Earth's natural resources, the optimization of the ongoing planetary ecocide, the relative maximization of the pleasures and profits enjoyed by the "civilized," whiter races of humanity and their proxies and redeemers. "Managed depletion" is, of course, a better course for Euro-Atlantic Western civilization to follow than the course of reckless depletion that it has followed heretofore, but managed depletion is depletion nonetheless, and what the vast majority wants and needs in order to survive is renewal and recreation.

Many of us are desperately in search of guidance on what is to be done, the most desperate among us being those of us who have lived most of our lives in the networks of "Global Cities" that are the strongholds of "human, all too human" civilizations. Having never lived without them, many of us have no clue how we might even begin to deconstruct and desert such civilizations. We feel clumsy and daft when handling the remnants of ancestral TEK that have survived the advance of the "human, all too human" model. We doubt that we have what it takes to (re-)construct ancestral TEK and (re-)create more-than-human societies anew. Our difficulty, however, is less that we do not know what to do and how to do it, than that we are afraid of what it will take to find out. We are afraid of so many inevitable failures and their consequences.

But shouldn't we be far more afraid of the consequences of never trying, never failing, and never learning from failure? Above all else, what we need to do, if we are to survive, is to learn from our own and others' failures and to teach others how to learn from failure. Ay, and this is precisely what TEK, properly understood, is all about. What differentiates ancestral TEK savvy from modern technology is not the fact that TEK involves mythical cosmogonies and ritual performances that are "unscientific" — the makings of TEK are, in fact, no less scientific than the makings of the technosphere. Rather, the difference is that TEK savvy empirical investigations and theoretical speculations are bound up with more-than-human mythical cosmogonies and ritual performances. The engineering of the technosphere, by contrast, assumes mythical cosmogonies and ritual performances that are "human, all too human," that make Man out to be the measure of all things.

Perhaps the most remarkable blows that have been struck by the "human, all too human" civilizations of the Euro-Atlantic West against primitive peoples have been the ideological blows that have sought to slander ancestral TEK and reduce it to no more than the unscientific and superstitious musings of primitive peoples. This repressive and ruinous fabrication was undertaken at immense cost of psychic and intellectual energies in the Euro-Atlantic West. But this expenditure was obligatory for the maintenance and advancement of "human, all too human" social arrangements centered in the Euro-Atlantic West.

It was by no means innocent. Consider the more obviously willful example of Spanish conquistadors, who dismissed indigenous peoples of Abya Yala, Anahuac, and Turtle Island as heathens, to be exploited and/or eliminated after simply reading the Requerimiento to them, without ever bothering to translate, provide cultural context, and learn the indigenous peoples' perspectives. But then consider how like Spanish conquistadors are the Western(ized) scientists, rarely bothering to question whether their own languages, customs, and belief systems are provincial, and so failing to entertain the possibility of deferring to non-Western(ized) others' languages, customs, and belief systems. Like Spanish conquistadors who willfully refused to commune with non-Western(ized) others in order to conquer their lands and stake claims to their natural resources, Western(ized) scientists willfully refuse to commune with non-Western(ized) others in order to conquer their minds and stake claims to their intellectual resources. Like the Spanish conquistador's relationship to conquered lands and natural resources, the Western(ized) scientist's relationship to conquered minds and intellectual resources is extractive as opposed to regenerative.

Today, just as the reckless depletion of natural resources is now yielding to their managed depletion, the reckless depletion of cultural resources is now yielding to the managed depletion of the same. Many Western(ized) scientists will now admit that ancestral TEK cannot be carelessly tossed aside as "unscientific," but these Western(ized) scientists do not believe that this is reason to invest in the substantive renewal and revitalization of ancestral TEK. Rather to the contrary, Western(ized) scientists consider this reason to invest in extracting the "hard science" from ancestral TEK, so that it can be exploited for the purposes of maintaining and advancing "human, all too human" social arrangements — afterwards casting aside the more-than-human mythical cosmogonies and ritual performances that nurtured the "hard science" prior to its being extracted from TEK.

To recognize that TEK involves science, without making any derisive qualifications, is to recognize that the only proper way for us to (re-)construct ancestral TEK anew is to conduct experiments that aim to (re-)create more-than-human mythical cosmogonies and ritual performances, to better nourish dynamic cultures in the here and now. Perfect adherence to the stories and strictures of static cultures that never actually existed has only ever been a demand imposed by civilized peoples on those peoples who have resisted the advances of "human, all too human" civilizations. Such peoples have always been dynamic, never static; they are forever (re-)creating themselves and their cultures anew, reworking the mythical cosmogonies and ritual performances that have been handed down to them. Failure and change have been the life breath of more-than-human cultures, the inhale and the exhale. Without failure and change, ancestral TEK suffocates and dies. To demand that primitive peoples prove their authenticity by strictly adhering to unchanging stories and strictures is, in fact, to demand that primitive peoples commit cultural suicide by suffocating their ancestral TEK.

All primitivisms are, properly speaking, neo-primitivisms inasmuch as all primitivisms are (re-)created anew each and every time that they are invoked and instantiated. What's more, all primitive peoples are neo-primitives inasmuch as all primitive peoples are forever (re-)creating themselves anew. Outmoded primitivisms and outmoded primitives are but self-serving figments of the "human, all too human" imagination, projected onto us in order to dispossess and denigrate us. When fear overtakes us, let us endeavor to overcome this fear by reminding ourselves and others that the failures of (neo-)primitive peoples tend to keep problems open to many different solutions, and that the achievements of civilized peoples tend toward that one and final solution, total destruction.

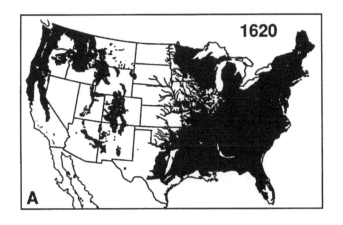

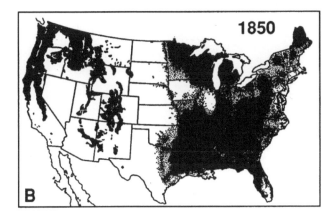

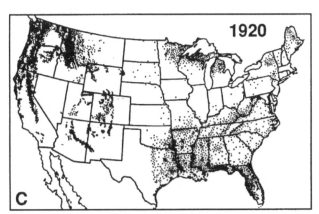

The deforestation of Turtle Island by the United Settlers of Amerikkka 1620-1920
Maps compiled by William B. Greeley, chief of the United Settler Forest Service from 1920 to 1928,
in his 1925 book The Relation of Geography to Timber Supply.

Select All | Clear All

☑ Potential forests
☑ Intact forests
☐ Extant 'wilds'

Conviviality

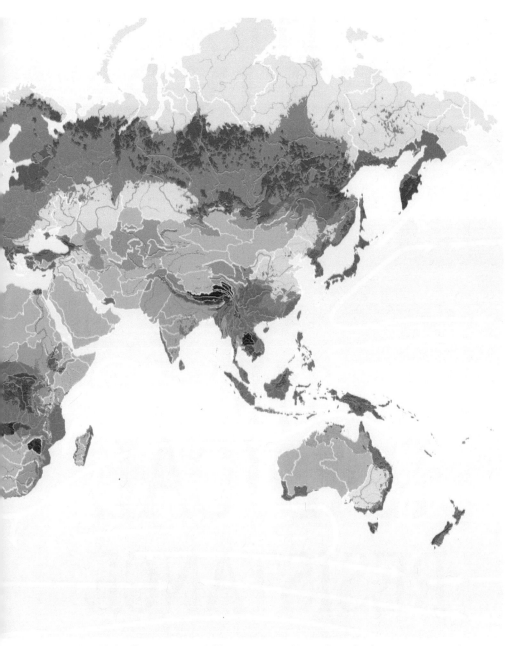

From TwinKillers.org , potential forest extent and intact forest landscapes, extant as of 2020, overlain atop the freshwater ecoregions of the world.

THE
RULING
CLASS
&
THE
RADICAL
RESISTANCE

Every imperialism is an endeavor to construct a stable and enduring power formation.

Stable and enduring power formations stratify societies. Not only do they filter and channel differing social elements apart from one another — the masculine from the feminine, the Black from the white, the developed from the underdeveloped, the human from the non-human, the living from the dead — they also make it increasingly burdensome and unappealing for differing social elements to commune fluently with one another, and more practical and appealing for some social elements to dominate, exploit, and eliminate others.

Every counterpower is an anti-imperialist movement that destabilizes and dissipates a power formation and destratifies a society. Counterpowers create confluences of differing social elements, making it increasingly more practical and more appealing for differing social elements to commune fluently with one another — for the masculine to commune fluently with the feminine, the Black with the white, the developed with the underdeveloped, the human with the non-human, the living with the dead. The more confluences that are enabled by counterpowers, the less determinate the differing social elements involved in so many confluences will become. This does not mean that confluent social elements will become more alike and differ less from one another — counterpowers do not diminish the differences between the Black and the white by making everything and everyone gray. Rather to the contrary, it means that confluent social elements will defer to one another more and more despite differing from one another — counterpowers confound attempts to filter and channel Blackness apart from whiteness by entangling the one with the other and creating confusion whenever and wherever attempts are made to disentangle them.

Imperialisms stratify societies by restricting the fundamental freedoms extended to differing social elements according to determinate logics that assign more freedoms to some elements and less to others. Counterpowers, in turn, destratify societies by extending fundamental freedoms further and further to increasingly more and increasingly different social elements according to an indeterminate logic. Thinking with and through the work of David Graeber and David Wengrow, there are three fundamental freedoms that are of greatest concern in this regard: (i) the freedom to flee, to migrate, move away or relocate from one's surroundings; (ii) the freedom to rebel, to ignore or disobey directives issued by others; and (iii) the freedom to (de-/re-)construct worlds, to shape entirely new social realities, or shift back and forth between different ones.

Today's prevailing imperialism is a white-supremacist capitalist patriarchal power formation that enables white men profitably engaged in capitalist relations of production to enjoy the fewest restrictions on their fundamental freedoms, while Black and indigenous women engaged in providing for social subsistence suffer the greatest restrictions on their fundamental freedoms. For social elements betwixt and between these extremes, the logic of white-supremacist capitalist patriarchy runs as follows: less restrictions are placed on the freedoms of all those who effectively serve as proxies and redeemers for rich white men, while more restrictions are placed on the fundamental freedoms of those who are either unwilling or unable to effectively serve rich white men. Those who provide the highest quality of service as proxies and redeemers, the "talented tenth," effectively become honorary rich white men and face the fewest restrictions by far, while those others who are the least willing and least able to serve as proxies and redeemers face restrictions similar to those faced by poor Black and indigenous women.

Concatenations of ruling powers, disciplinary powers, normalizing powers, and optimizing powers effect the logic of white-supremacist capitalist patriarchy.

Ruling powers today enact ritualized spectacles that exaggerate the "achievements" of rich white men, their proxies, and their redeemers, enabling them to feel "superior" to others. The ritualized spectacles involved in maintaining and mobilizing police and military forces to restrict the freedoms of non-whites are amongst the most important in this regard.

Disciplinary powers today enact routine examinations that enable rich white men, their proxies, and their redeemers to transform their feelings regarding the "inferiority" of others into prevailing standards and stereotypes. The routine examinations used by teachers evaluating pupils in schools, by bosses evaluating employees in workplaces, and social workers evaluating people in line for social services are amongst the most important in this regard.

Normalizing powers today enact biased surveys that transform prevailing standards and stereotypes that presume the "inferiority" of others into technical/

statistical facts. The biased surveys conducted by the social scientists and technocrats who shape public policy are amongst the most important in this regard.

Optimizing powers today enact variable controls that employ technical/statistical facts regarding the "inferiority" of others to compel others to adopt "best practices" and "measure up" to the "superior" standards of achievement set by rich white men, their proxies, and their redeemers. The variable controls deployed by social engineers, management consultants, public relations professionals and other social cyberneticians are amongst the most enabling in this regard.

The concatenations of ruling powers, disciplinary powers, normalizing powers, and optimizing powers that constitute today's imperial order are overseen and managed by a ruling class formed of those individuals who hold the most important decision-making positions in the most heavily-armed police and military units ("we shoot at you"), the best endowed academic institutions and philanthropic organizations ("we fool you"), and the wealthiest national governments and transnational corporations ("we rule you"). The individuals who form this ruling class ostensibly face the fewest restrictions on their fundamental freedoms but, here is the rub, they are also those who have proven themselves the best risks for the prevailing imperial order, having been filtered and channeled into their positions of authority by the workings of the very same ruling, disciplinary, normalizing, and optimizing powers described above. This is to say, in other words, that those who are able to exercise the greatest degree of freedom under the prevailing imperial order also tend to be those who are least likely to exercise their freedom in a manner that threatens the prevailing imperial order.

We too often attribute more agency to the members of the ruling class than is deserved. The reality is that decisions made at the helms of the organs of Empire that shoot us, fool us, and rule us are, to quote the authors of the journal Chuang (闯), "always decisions made in response to material limits confronted by complex political and economic systems." Indeed, it is worth quoting the authors of Chuang at length on this matter:

> The ruling class is a designator for a non-homogeneous array of individuals who hold decision-making positions within the citadels of political-economic power, for whom the continuation of the status quo is of the utmost priority. But these individuals sit in highly structured positions, beholden to the built-in demands of shareholders (for higher profit) and political constituencies (for minimal levels of stability and prosperity, not so much the requirement that things get better but

simply that they don't get too bad too fast). There is thus no real malicious intent behind [their] decisions, nor is there the ability for such holders of power to truly transform or break free from the system itself. They are chained to it just as we all are, though they find themselves chained to its top. The entire process [of maintaining and advancing the prevailing imperial order] is [...] one of contingent adaptations, rather than ruling class conspiracy. [The maintenance and advancement of the prevailing imperial order] is therefore not a fully conscious, casually malicious political program, as some authors would have it, but simply a term attributed to a loose consensus formed around numerous local solutions to [crises] that seemed to overcome short-term limits at the time [of their formulation].

The authors of Chuang, otherwise on point, neglect to mention something important: the chains that bind those at the top of the system tend to be far more subjective and psychological and far less objective and physical. Simply put, those at the top are, above all else, "trauma bound" to their positions of privilege. By contrast, those at the bottom, in addition to being trauma bound to their positions of servitude, are also bound by the reality that they and their loved ones would be deprived of food, shelter, and other basic necessities if they were to desert their positions of servitude.

The ruling class is, in sum, a fractious group of individuals who are trauma bound to threatened positions of privilege, and they are always desperately grasping for motives, means, and opportunities to overcome threats to their positions of privilege. What we call imperialist white-supremacist capitalist patriarchy is not the result of a well thought out elite conspiracy. Rather to the contrary, it is the accretion of five-centuries of desperate and hasty marriages of convenience that have enabled Euro-Atlantic elites to maintain and advance the privileges to which they are trauma bound.

Euro-Atlantic elites deny this. They rationalize their desperate and hasty marriages of convenience by wrapping them up in ideological and mythical narratives. They claim that some combination of natural superiority, divine dispensation, and/or historical necessity brought them to power, and they argue that their opponents and subordinates have been on the wrong side of Nature, God, and/or History. The truth is that elite decision-makers are always and forever (i) reacting to their fear of losing privileges to which they are trauma bound and then, subsequently, (ii) covering up the fact that they are reacting out of fear. In an essay titled "Let Us Think About Fear", John Berger forcefully asserted this reality:

*Any of us can become terrified at any moment if fear waylays us. The leaders of [Empire],
however, would seem to be married to Fear, and their subordinate Commanders and Sergeants
to be indoctrinated from above with something of the same fear.*

*What are the practices of this marriage? Day and night the partners of Fear are anx-
iously preoccupied with telling themselves and their subordinates the right half-truths, half-truths
which hope to change the world from what it is into something which it is not! It takes about six
half-truths to make a lie. As a result, they become unfamiliar with reality, whilst continuing
to dream about, and of course to exercise, power. They continually have to absorb shocks whilst
accelerating. Decisiveness becomes their invariable device for preventing the asking of questions.*

The ruling class is desperately afraid of being questioned. It is not just that
they fear being questioned by those over whom they rule but, more profoundly
still, they also fear that they might start questioning themselves. Thus the ruling
class is always claiming that their bold and decisive decision-making is urgently
needed.

Radical resistance to imperialism begins with the realization that bold and
decisive decision-making is not urgently needed, rather, what is urgently needed
is time for convivial forms of questioning and experimentation. Those who argue
that the forces of resistance must yield (to) bold and decisive decision-makers are
those who are only interested in resistance as a means to reform and restructure
the existing ruling class. By contrast, a radical resistance seeks to abolish the need
for a ruling class, as opposed to reforming and restructuring an existing ruling class.

¡Que se vayan todos! All of them must go!

The crucial privilege to which the ruling class desperately clings is that of
knowing that more freedoms are extended to them than to those beneath
them. What the ruling class wants above all else is to restrict the extension of
freedoms to those beneath them so as to maintain their relative advantages. The
ruling class is fine with having fewer and fewer freedoms extended to them in
absolute terms as long as they have more and more freedoms extended to them
relative to those beneath them.

A radical resistance to imperialism is all about extending the freedoms to
flee, rebel, and (de-/re-)construct worlds to the maximum extent possible. Contra
the ruling class, a radical resistance assumes that fundamental freedoms do not
need to be earned. Instead, what has to be "earned" is the power to restrict the
fundamental freedoms of others. Furthermore, a radical resistance holds that

the power to restrict others' fundamental freedoms cannot be "earned" without the continuous and freely given consent of those whose fundamental freedoms are being restricted. This is to say, in other words, that fundamental freedoms ought only to be restricted by and through the workings of a continuous consensus process — which is neither a discrete consent form nor a discrete polling forum but, rather, a continuous conversation that (re-)negotiates the dissensus within an overall consensus and the consensus within an overall dissensus. From the perspective of a radical resistance, all authorities who exercise powers that limit others' freedoms to flee, rebel, and remake social realities are exercising unearned privileges to the degree that they do so without facilitating a continuous consensus process.

A radical anti-imperialist resistance can form itself whenever and wherever it is possible to challenge the unearned privileges of prevailing authorities by and through initiating a continuous consensus process. Continuous consensus processes are endeavors to make it increasingly more practical and more appealing for differing social elements to commune fluently with one another and, as such, all effective continuous consensus processes form counterpowers.

The prevailing imperial order is overseen and managed by a ruling class of decision-makers who exercise unearned privileges to restrict peoples' fundamental freedoms at many different points in time and space. A radical resistance must think strategically and conduct experiments in order to discover which places and times are most vulnerable to acts of radical resistance that effect continuous consensus processes, and, further, which of these vulnerable points are confluent with other such points nearby in space and time such that contagion is possible amongst them. Michel Foucault recognized something like this when he wrote:

The points, knots, or focuses of resistance are spread over time and space at varying densities, at times mobilizing groups or individuals in a definitive way, inflaming certain points of the body, certain moments of life, certain types of behavior. Are there no great radical ruptures, massive binary divisions, then? Occasionally, yes. But more often one is dealing with mobile and transitory points of resistance, producing cleavages in a society that shift about, fracturing unities and effecting regroupings, furrowing across individuals themselves, cutting them up and remolding them, marking off irreducible regions in them, in their bodies and minds. Just as the network of power relations ends by forming a dense web that passes through apparatuses and institutions, without being exactly localized in them, so too the swarm of points of resistance traverses social stratifications and individual unities. And it is doubtless the strategic codification of these points of resistance that makes a revolution possible.

Wherever and whenever a radical resistance decides to initiate a continuous consensus process, one will find the ruling class complaining (i) that continuous consensus processes are an ineffective and inefficient way to make decisions and (ii) that we are facing crises that demand swift and effective decision making and expert decision makers. What the ruling class fails to acknowledge, of course, is that it is their decisions that have caused those crises, and that they have made them in order to ensure that there is an ever increasing demand for swift and effective decision making by expert decision makers. Privileged decision-makers will make a spectacle of wanting to avoid crises but, in actuality, they invariably get off on producing and managing crises; they scrupulously precipitate crises that create a demand for their decision-making powers. What a radical resistance aims to do, above all else, is to break the cycle.

We all know, for instance, that climate change did not have to become the crisis that it is now. Indeed, the fact of the matter is this: the ruling class, consciously or unconsciously, sought to make climate change into a crisis because they sensed that a climate crisis would empower them further. Indeed, when climate change was first recognized, there were many ways to respond to climate change that did not involve placing further restrictions on oppressed peoples' freedoms to flee, to rebel and to (de-/re-)construct worlds. Climate change had to be made into an urgent crisis if the ruling class was to use it as an excuse to further restrict oppressed peoples' freedoms relative to the freedoms enjoyed by the ruling class. Knowing this, consciously or unconsciously, the ruling class made decisions that resulted in climate change becoming the crisis that it is at present. Now that the climate crisis is upon us, many in the ruling class feel that the time is ripe to declare a climate emergency so that they may enjoy the privilege of exercising emergency powers.

The great irony here is that there is no halting the climate crisis without depriving the most privileged decision-makers, those who rule over the most people and places, of their decision making powers. Climate change is a global phenomenon, of course, but its character is such that any and all effective responses to it will be hyperlocal. This is because the global phenomenon that is climate change is only the aggregate statistical result of so many hyperlocal changes. Our societies are presently failing to respond to climate change effectively because decisions about how to respond are being made by regional and global authorities who are incapable of responding to so many ongoing hyperlocal changes as they occur, and who must react to aggregate statistical results and catastrophic events that are indexes of hyperlocal changes that have already run their course.

Ay, the climate crisis is but a part of the most wicked problem ever created by privileged decision makers, a problem that privileged decision makers simply cannot solve from their positions of privilege: the problem of countering the twin scourges of global apartheid and planetary ecocide before it is too late.

GDP per capita, 1974 to 2018

This data is adjusted for inflation and for differences in the cost of living between countries.

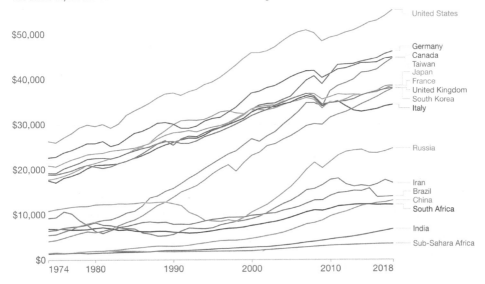

Source: Maddison Project Database 2020 (Bolt and van Zanden, 2020)
Note: This data is expressed in international-$ at 2011 prices.

Poverty: Share of population living on less than $10 a day, 1974 to 2020

This data is adjusted for inflation and for differences in the cost of living between countries.

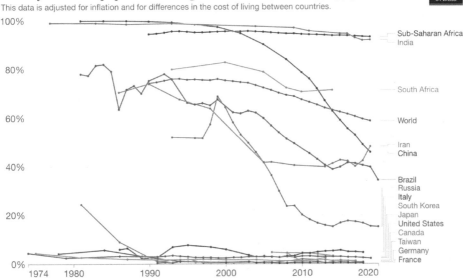

Source: World Bank Poverty and Inequality Platform
Note: This data is measured in international-$ at 2017 prices. Depending on the country and year, it relates to either disposable income or consumption per capita.

Figure 4: Number of US dollar millionaires (% of world total) by country, 2021

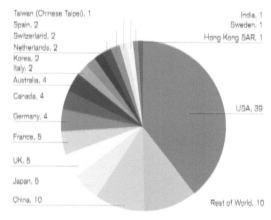

Taiwan (Chinese Taipei), 1
Spain, 2
Switzerland, 2
Netherlands, 2
Korea, 2
Italy, 2
Australia, 4
Canada, 4
Germany, 4
France, 5
UK, 5
Japan, 5
China, 10

India, 1
Sweden, 1
Hong Kong SAR, 1

USA, 39

Rest of World, 10

Source: James Davies, Rodrigo Lluberas and Anthony Shorrocks, Credit Suisse Global Wealth Databook 2022

Wealth per adult across countries

An overall perspective on the disparity of wealth across countries and regions is captured by the World Wealth Map (**Figure 5**). It shows that nations with high wealth per adult (above USD 100,000) are concentrated in North America and Western Europe, and among the richer parts of East Asia, the Pacific and the Middle East, with a sprinkling of outposts in the Caribbean. China and Russia are core members of the "intermediate wealth" group of countries with mean wealth in the range of USD 25,000–100,000. This group also includes more recent members of the European Union and important emerging-market economies in Latin America and the Middle East. One step below, the "frontier wealth" range of USD 5,000–25,000 per adult is a heterogeneous group that covers heavily populated countries such as India, Indonesia and the Philippines, plus most of South America and leading sub-Saharan nations such as South Africa. Fast-developing Asian countries like Cambodia, Laos and Vietnam also fall within this category. Countries with average wealth below USD 5,000 comprise the final group, which is dominated by countries in central Africa.

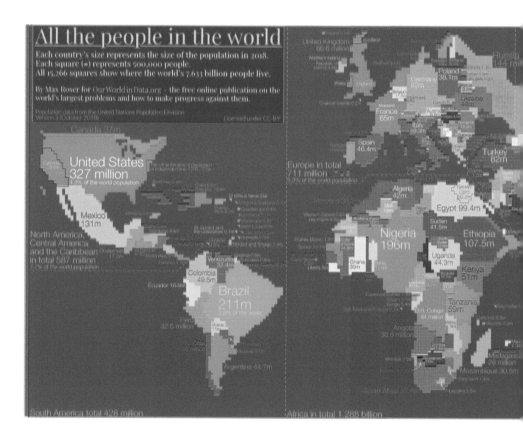

Figure 5: World Wealth Map 2021

Wealth levels (USD)

Below USD 5,000
USD 5,000 to 25,000
USD 25,000 to 100,000
Over USD 100,000

Source: James Davies, Rodrigo Lluberas and Anthony Shorrocks, Credit Suisse Global Wealth Databook 2022

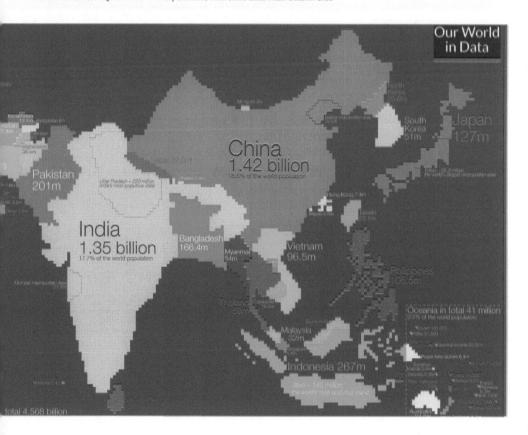

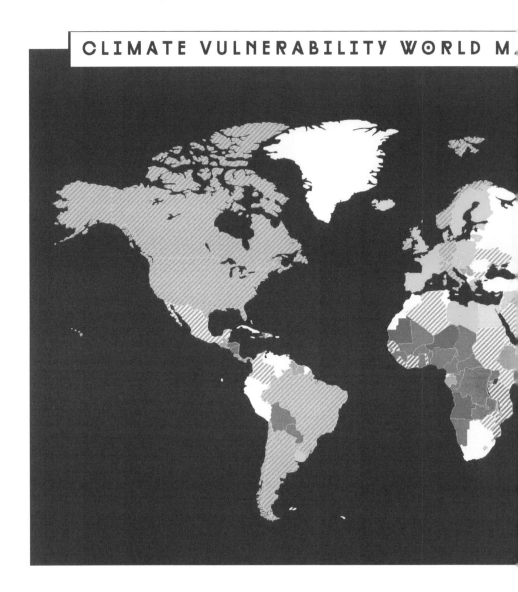

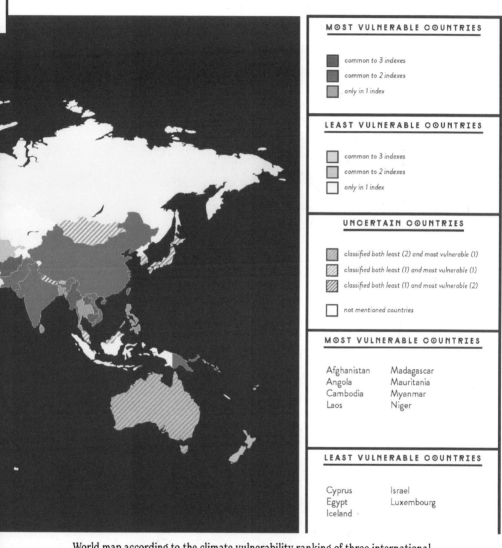

MOST VULNERABLE COUNTRIES

- common to 3 indexes
- common to 2 indexes
- only in 1 index

LEAST VULNERABLE COUNTRIES

- common to 3 indexes
- common to 2 indexes
- only in 1 index

UNCERTAIN COUNTRIES

- classified both least (2) and most vulnerable (1)
- classified both least (1) and most vulnerable (1)
- classified both least (1) and most vulnerable (2)
- not mentioned countries

MOST VULNERABLE COUNTRIES

Afghanistan	Madagascar
Angola	Mauritania
Cambodia	Myanmar
Laos	Niger

LEAST VULNERABLE COUNTRIES

Cyprus	Israel
Egypt	Luxembourg
Iceland	

World map according to the climate vulnerability ranking of three international Indexes (DARA, German Watch, Gain). The striped countries are considered vulnerable by some indexes and safe by others, indicating the uncertainty in the general climate debate. By Carlo De Gaetano, Stefania Guerra, Gabriele Colombo.

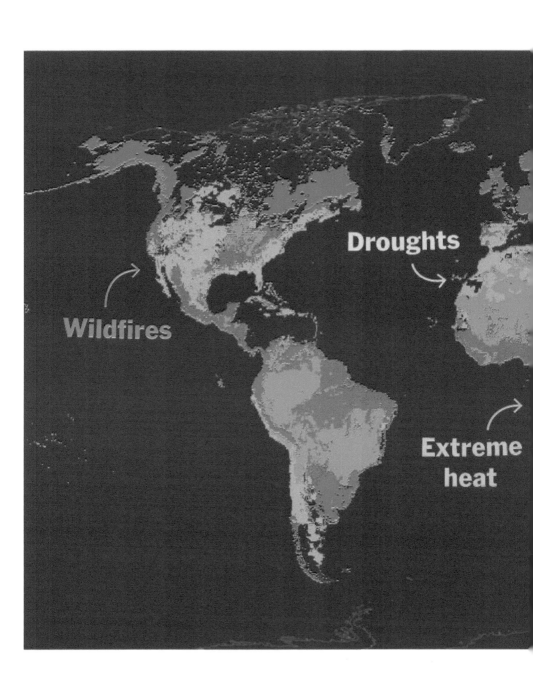

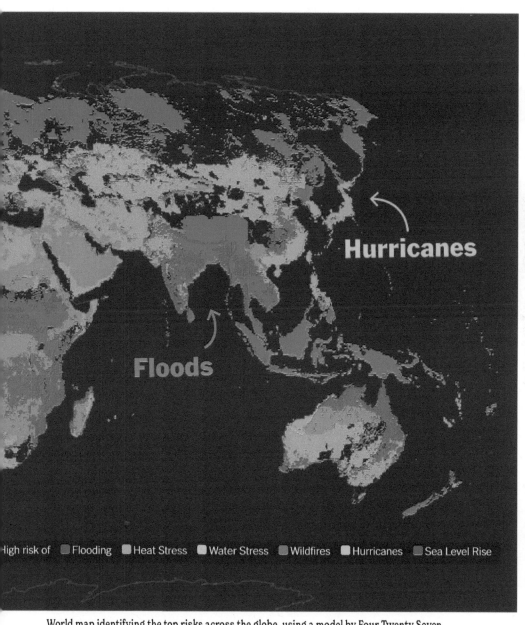

Hurricanes

Floods

High risk of ■ Flooding   ■ Heat Stress   ■ Water Stress   ■ Wildfires   ■ Hurricanes   ■ Sea Level Rise

World map identifying the top risks across the globe, using a model by Four Twenty Seven, a company that analyzes climate risks. By Yaryna Serkez for the New York Times.

ANTI-COLONIALISM, ANTI-RACISM, & ECOLOGY

Asked in a recent interview whether or not ecology can and should be the common cause that unites the world today, a well-known white European philosopher, Jacques Rancière, responded as follows:

Rather than opening up a new horizon of hope, ecology presents us with an imminent catastrophe. To the 'there is no alternative' of capitalist necessity, hammered into us by our governments, it opposes another logic of urgent necessity: the race to save the planet. We are told this is the only thing to do. But the question is: who will do it? Most environmentalist discourses want to overcome the old political divisions by stating the conditions for the planet's survival, but, in this way, they short-circuit the question of the political subject: what fighting forces, what forms of struggle can make ecology the cause of all and not that of experts who rely on the goodwill of the masters of the world?

In other words, this white European philosopher is willing to concede that countering planetary ecocide is a "common cause" for people across the globe to rally around today, but he is skeptical as to whether those promoting the cause have answered the question of who will "lead" the cause and who will "follow."

It is a mark of Rancière's white Eurocentricity that he hasn't recognized that his question has already been asked and definitively answered by radicals hailing from the Black, indigenous, and colored communities of the global majority. Simply put, the movement to counter ecocide must be led by radicals belonging to the dispossessed and denigrated races of humanity in communion with non-human others — those for whom ecological catastrophe is not an imminent threat but the accomplished fact of white Eurocentric humanism. Only anti-colonial and anti-racist fighting forces and forms of struggle can make countering ecocide the cause of all, and these forces must be cooperatively led by those most victimized by colonialism and racism.

On the one hand, though the global cause of ecology must be cooperatively led by the dispossessed victims of colonialism in general, it is important for the cause to defer to the victims of settler colonialism in particular: the indigenous peoples whose homelands were stolen from them by white European settlers bent on driving indigenous peoples and their cultures to extinction.

On the other hand, though the global cause of ecology must be cooperatively led by the denigrated victims of racism in general, it is important for the cause to defer to the victims of anti-Black racism in particular: the African peoples cast as socially dead, slave stock to be harvested and deported from their homelands by white European colonizers bent on breeding a slave labor force composed of dark-skinned peoples minted "Negroes."

Eurocentric humanists have, to a large extent, failed to recognize and defer to Black and indigenous peoples as leading political subjects in global rebellions and resistance movements against the ecocidal machinations of the imperialist white-supremacist capitalist patriarchal world order. Too many believe, like Karl Marx did, that the white working classes and white youth of the Euro-Atlantic's most "advanced" civilizations have been and will continue to be at the forefront of global rebellions and resistance movements against a capitalism that they imagine can be disentangled from racism, sexism, and humanism. Too many are oblivious to the fact that, for more than five hundred years, the white working classes and white youth of the Euro-Atlantic's most advanced civilizations have been making deadly and disastrous compromises with global capitalism at the expense of the victims of colonialism and racism, all while the victims of colonialism and racism have instigated and led the most creative rebellions and resistance movements against capitalism. Indeed, the white working classes and white youth of the Euro-Atlantic have only ever been agents of radical change when they have taken the side of and learned from the examples of the victims of colonialism and racism. They have, otherwise, been reactionary forces: either siding with capitalists against the victims of colonialism and racism or turning a blind eye to the suffering of these victims.

This is not to say that the white working classes and white youth of the Euro-Atlantic have no positive role to play in radical peoples' movements to counter ecocide today. Rather to the contrary, this is to say that the white working classes and white youth need to learn to play accompanying and supporting roles. Every maker and connoisseur of the performing arts knows better than to dismiss the role of the accompaniment and the supporting players involved in a performance, for it is very often the quality of the accompaniment and the supporting players that makes or breaks the performances of the leading players. Who would the great Motown stars be without the remarkable session players who accompanied and supported them on their records and tours?

With this in mind, ecologically-minded segments of the white working classes and white youth of the Euro-Atlantic ought to be asking themselves the following question, "How can we rebel against our bosses and our elders in such a way that we are effectively accompanying and supporting anti-colonial and anti-racist struggles led by Black and indigenous peoples?" In and through asking and answering this question, the white working classes and white youth will learn to attend to the histories and follow the currents of anti-colonial and anti-racist struggles, and to get a feel for the rhythms and patterns of these struggles so that they might accompany them in complementary ways by and through fighting class and generational struggles.

Going further and digging deeper, this does not mean that the white working classes and white youth need to take orders from the victims of colonialism and racism but, rather, that they need to both cue in and take cues from them. In keeping with figures of leadership found in performing ensembles, as opposed to figures found in bureaucratic hierarchies, the player who takes the lead in an ensemble performance isn't a "decision-maker" who gives orders to the other players. Rather, the lead player is a "focal point" where cues from different members of the ensemble gather and from where divergent cues to different members of the ensemble disperse.

No matter whether we are Black, white, indigenous, or colored, and no matter whether our ancestors identified with the colonizers or their victims, we must all be wary of those who vigorously take up the cause of ecology today without also taking up the histories and currents of anti-colonial and anti-racist struggles with equal vigor. A global ecology movement that cannot be recognized as an anti-colonial and anti-racist movement, and that does not invite Black and indigenous rebels to play leading roles, is an eco-imperialist ruse.

Imperialist white-supremacist capitalist patriarchs have dominated the world stage for centuries, conducting genocides, ethnocides, and ecocides in the name of civilization and progress, and violently forcing darker peoples into subordinate roles as their proxies, redeemers, and slaves. Today, agents of the white-savior industrial complex of Empire are posing as experts and leaders on matters of sustainability and conservation, and they are claiming that the future of civilization and progress demands that they be granted new powers and authorities to administer and supervise the lives of the victims of colonialism and racism. The new found mission of white saviors, the "white man's burden" of the New Eco-Imperialism, is to intervene in the lives of poor Black, indigenous, and colored peoples in order to teach them the virtues of sustainability and conservation.

Returning to where we began, we must wonder why Eurocentric thinkers like Rancière are so reluctant to openly recognize the past and present leadership of Black, indigenous, and other colored peoples in global rebellions and resistance movements against the ecocidal machinations of Empire. Such reluctance suggests that these Eurocentric thinkers are priming the white working classes and white youth of the Euro-Atlantic West to make a deadly and disastrous compromise with the New Eco-Imperialists at the expense of the victims of colonialism and racism. To this end, Eurocentric thinkers are choosing to engage in the fabrication and fabulation of a radical "people-to-come" from out of the white working classes and white youth of Europe and Amerikkka. These fabrications and fabulations deny the reality that the white working classes and white youth cannot become radical forces for reparative and regenerative change without first recognizing and supporting the leadership of Black, indigenous, and other colored rebels who simply cannot self-actualize and become who they are apart from becoming radical forces for change.

THE
FETISHES
OF EMPIRE

I do not hold fast to the notion that the capitalists' so-called "profit motive" is to blame for our social ills today.

I believe that the profit motive is the most prevalent deathly rationalization of many of our social ills, yes, but I don't believe that the rationalization of a toxic pattern of behavior fully explains the toxic pattern of behavior. The rationalization only ever indexes the pleasure that the toxic pattern of behavior yields.

Those who focus exclusively on the (ir)rationality of the profit motive are falling for a clever ruse. Uncover the ruse and one discovers social forms and practices of enculturation that privilege men who take pleasure in denigrating and dispossessing others, especially othered women and, writ large, (Mother) Nature as an othered woman by analogy.

All endeavors to do away with imperialist white-supremacist capitalist patriarchy by analyzing the profit motive are a lost cause. There is no countering imperialist white-supremacist capitalist patriarchy without countering the social forms and practices of enculturation that enable men to derive pleasure from exercising the power to denigrate and dispossess.

Too few recognize and fewer are brave enough to teach others that the maintenance and advancement of imperialist white-supremacist capitalist patriarchy has always been about toxic masculine pleasure seeking. Many cruel happenings since the years 1444 and 1492 only make sense if one attends to the fetishistic pleasures that they satisfied and the fetishists that they implicate: the capitalist, the white supremacist, and the slave master.

The exemplary capitalist is a patriarch whose socially constructed "endowments" enable them to exploit women threatened with poverty. They either use their endowments for their own direct pleasure, or take indirect pleasure lording them over others, brandishing their stockpiles of wealth like an oversized phallus.

The exemplary white supremacist is a patriarch whose socially constructed "endowments" enable them to exploit women threatened by projects of racial and cultural extermination, by genocide and ethnocide. They either use their endowments for their own direct pleasure, or take indirect pleasure lording them over others, brandishing their means of mass slaughter and cultural erasure like an oversized phallus.

The exemplary slave master is a patriarch whose socially constructed "endowments" enable them to exploit women in bondage and captivity. They either use their endowments for their own direct pleasure, or take indirect pleasure lording them over others, brandishing their retinues of docile bodies like an oversized phallus.

Wherever an imperialist white-supremacist capitalist patriarchal regime has prevailed, the profit motive has served to rationalize the pleasurable fetishistic ends noted above, it has never been an end in itself. Ay, the iconography of every such regime has always functioned like an oversized dick pic.

To properly grasp the deeply interlocked horrors of white-supremacy, capitalism, and patriarchy, we must call out the fact that, at bottom, those who call themselves "white men" and those who serve white men as proxies and redeemers get off on the reproduction of Black women in bondage as captives for their direct pleasure, and the reproduction of Black men in bondage as captives for their indirect pleasure. Extracting labor from Black bodies only ever served to rationalize the reproduction of captives to please white men: cheap labor is the byproduct of racialized slavery and apartheid, not the primary product.

Racialized slave labor was never the cheapest to obtain and maintain, nor the easiest to find and keep, nor the most efficient form of labor. Rather to the contrary, racialized slave labor was always a perversely expensive and pleasurable luxury. In other words, the pleasure to be found in racialized slavery was not in the productive use of Black bodies but in the pleasurable wasting of Black bodies. Laborers who can read, write, think for themselves, and take initiative are far more productive and profitable than workers who must be constrained and surveilled at all times to ensure that they do not read, write, think for themselves, nor take initiative.

The most outrageous lie that we are taught in school is that the enslavement of Africans by Christian Europeans was a practical solution to a real labor shortage problem. The labor shortage problem was not real and, even if it were real, enslaving Africans was not a practical solution. In actuality, Christian Europeans envied the ostentatious luxury of the Islamic kingdoms that they warred with, including their retinues of slaves, and they sought to both emulate and outdo their Islamic rivals by accumulating similar such luxuries. Of course, slaves were put to work and made to produce useful and profitable goods and services, but such "practical uses" of slaves were byproducts of the impractical luxury of being able to command others to do one's bidding and to destroy their bodies, minds, and spirits in the process.

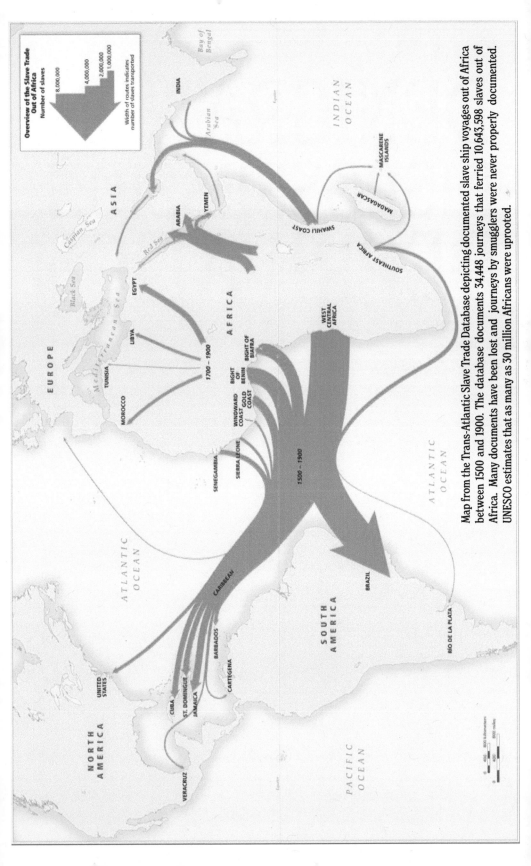

Map from the Trans-Atlantic Slave Trade Database depicting documented slave ship voyages out of Africa between 1500 and 1900. The database documents 34,448 journeys that ferried 10,643,598 slaves out of Africa. Many documents have been lost and journeys by smugglers were never properly documented. UNESCO estimates that as many as 30 million Africans were uprooted.

Overview of the Slave Trade Out of Africa
Number of slaves

8,000,000
4,000,000
2,000,000
1,000,000

Width of routes indicates number of slaves transported

DENIGRATION, DISPOSSESSION, DEPRIVATION

Jettisoning the sorry Marxist concept and turn of phrase "primitive accumulation," as of late, I've been thinking with and through the phrase and concepts of "accumulation by denigration" and "accumulation by dispossession." Accumulation by denigration (from Latin *denigrare* "to blacken") being the modus operandi of anti-Black racism, and accumulation by dispossession being that of (settler) colonialism.

As rationalizations, accumulation by denigration and dispossession serve to plausibly justify acts that satisfy the fetishes of empire, on the one hand, and, on the other hand, render imperial harvests of fetishistic pleasures increasingly more bountiful and efficient, though still not always profitable.

Those who believe that capitalism turns on making profits are mistaken. Capitalism actually turns on rationalizing fetishistic pleasures to make them increasingly more economical. Asceticism in pursuit of the profit motive is the imposition that capitalist empires put upon their victims. The denigrated and the dispossessed are compelled to make themselves profitable or else meet an early death; while the denigrators and dispossessors compulsively pursue pleasure by driving their victims to early deaths, often by making it increasingly difficult for their victims to make themselves profitable.

Crises produced by the falling rate of profit are precisely what capitalists seek— they are excuses that the capitalists need to subject the bodies, minds, spirits, and lands of the dispossessed and denigrated to all sorts of punishing deprivations. Ay, this is capitalism in a nutshell: debtors must injure themselves more and more in order to become more and more profitable for their creditors and employers, or else their creditors and employers will have license to take pleasure in subjecting them to punishing deprivations.

Going further still, those who believe that capital accumulation, generally speaking, (re)produces deprivation are also mistaken. It is accumulation by dispossession that initially (re-)produces deprivation; then it is accumulation by denigration that disciplines and normalizes the (re-)production of deprivation; then, finally, all forms of capital accumulation apart from accumulation by dispossession and denigration only serve to optimize the (re-)production of deprivation — financialization and industrialization being chief amongst them.

In other words, dispossession forms the roots of deprivation; denigration forms the stems of deprivation; and financialization and industrialization form some of the leaves and fruits of deprivation. Those who focus their energies on decrying the excesses of finance and industry, without properly attending to matters of dispossession and denigration, are only interested in plucking the bitter leaves and sweet fruits off that toxic plant, leaving its roots and stems intact.

Deprivation is a tip rooting bramble. Dispossessions are at the root of all deprivations, yes, but denigrations are their tip-rooting thorny stems, issuing new roots when they touch down upon suitable ground.

Chief among the deepest and most enduring roots of modern deprivation are its settler colonial roots; and chief among those thorny stems of modern deprivation that have tipped over most prodigiously and generated new roots over and over again are its anti-Black stems. But the settler colonial roots of modern deprivation are by no means the only roots: consider, for instance, the dispossessions effected by the enclosure movements in Britain during the 18th and 19th centuries. Similarly, the anti-Black stems of modern deprivation are by no means the only stems: consider, for instance, how the social categories of religion and caste were reworked by the British colonial census bureau to further the denigration of sub-populations of Britain's colonized subjects in India.

Nevertheless, the settler colonial roots and anti-Black stems of modern deprivation are among the most well-established and fiercely opportunistic roots and stems. Those with any proximity to settler colonialism and anti-blackness must confront them directly if they seriously intend to confront and counter (post)modern deprivation. Those without proximity should confront similarly well-established and fiercely opportunistic roots and stems that are within their reach, like the enduring legacies of the enclosures in England and the caste system in India. Ay, we must all strike at and clear away such roots and stems or else be suffocated by them.

Rome - October 4, 2023

(SELF-) POSSESSION, (ANTI-) BLACKNESS, & ABOLITION

I found myself in Rome on September 25, 2022. It was election day and the Brothers of Italy (Fratelli d'Italia) — an anti-migrant nationalist party whose descent can be traced back to the original Fascist party — were on their way to winning the most seats in the Italian parliament.

Although the derivative fascists were winning parliament, if the prevailing street art was any indication of reality, they weren't necessarily winning the streets of Rome.

In several neighborhoods of Rome, individuals and groups who aspired to communistic ideals and practices of freedom had spray painted radical glyphs on the walls. Though not the most popular of these glyphs, there were two very familiar ones that regularly caught my eye: : "BLM", standing for Black Lives Matter, and "ACAB", standing for All Cops Are Bastards.

Inspired by these encounters this essay aims to articulate the relationship between chattel-slavery, wage-slavery, mass incarceration in the United Settler States; anti-migrant policies and global apartheid more broadly; and the worldwide prevalence of anti-Black power formations. I have been compelled to write on the topic because everything that I have read thus far on the topic has been less articulate than I would like. But this is no fault of the authors whom I have read on the topic: their texts are meant to become articulate by being read and responded to, and this is my response.

PART I. (SELF-)POSSESSION

I spent the morning of September 26th gazing at the ruins of the "human, all too human" Axial Age civilization of ancient Rome, the imperialist patriarchy and military-slavery-coinage complex that set so many templates within the Euro-Atlantic West, and inspired so many wet dreams of dominion. Surveying the archaeological sites, I imagined the spectacular cruelties and horrors that took place at the Colosseum, the pretenses of nobility at the Forum, and the ill-gotten luxuries of empire and slavery enjoyed atop the Palatine.

After I got back to my lodgings, I sat down to re-read passages from David Graeber and David Wengrow's remarkable book, *The Dawn of Everything*, in order to help me better understand the civilization whose ruins I had just surveyed, and to reckon with one of its most enduring legacies. Specifically, the ancient Roman Law conception of property that has come to inform the modern Euro-Atlantic conception of freedom as self-possession and, further, the distinction between the chattel-slave and the wage-slave — with the latter, the wage-slave, often termed the "free laborer" or "worker" in our prevailing doublespeak.

What makes the Roman Law conception of property – the basis of almost all legal systems today – unique is that the responsibility to care and share is reduced to a minimum, or even eliminated entirely. In Roman Law there are three basic rights relating to possession: usus *(the right to use),* fructus *(the right to enjoy the products of a property, for instance the fruit of a tree), and* abusus *(the right to damage or destroy). If one has only the first two rights this is referred to as* usufruct, *and is not considered true possession under the law. The defining feature of true legal property, then, is that one has the option of not taking care of it, or even destroying it at will.*

Today's wage-slave is someone in "full possession" of their own person. What the wage-slave sells to their employer in return for wages are temporary *usufruct* rights (*usus* and *fructus*) over their person under the terms of an explicit or implicit employment contract. The wage-slave retains their *abusus* rights for themself and themself alone. The legislation of wage-slavery, which is more typically called "labor law" in our prevailing doublespeak, is primarily concerned (i) with regulating the terms under which employers can purchase *usus* and *fructus* rights from wage-slaves (a.k.a. "employees" or "workers") and (ii) with determining the recourses that wage-slaves have to take action against employers who overstep the bounds of employment contracts and engage in *abusus* of wage-slaves. Thus when the unionized wage-slave limits their dreams of freedom to maximizing the recourses available to them to take action against their employer for trespassing upon their *abusus* rights, they still accept wage-slavery on its own terms.

The chattel-slave differs from the wage-slave in having been "fully dis-possessed" of their own person: slave-masters are entitled to *usus, fructus,* and *abusus* rights over their chattel-slaves unless and until their slaves are emancipated. Indeed, the legislation of chattel slavery is primarily concerned with enabling the slave-master to exercise their full rights, and especially their *abusus* rights, within limits established to prevent such exercise from harming public order and public health. Given this, those who conceive of reparations as payment of "back wages" for the *usus* and *fructus* of the chattel slave miss the point. The *abusus* of the chattel-slave was the condition of possibility for the *usus* and *fructus* of the chattel-slave, and reparations must acknowledge and make amends for the *abusus* of the chattel-slave as that which precedes, exceeds, and succeeds the *usus* and *fructus* of the chattel-slave. And yet, to make amends for the *abusus* of the chattel-slave without dispensing with conceptions of freedom as (self-)possession is also to miss the point.

There is, undoubtedly, some degree of salvation to be had in being a self-possessed wage-slave rather than a chattel-slave possessed by a slave-master. That being said, there is no denying the fact that extreme forms of corporal and symbolic violence are involved in the making and maintenance of both the wage-slave and the chattel-slave. What's more, the violence that makes and maintains the wage-slave cannot be disentangled from the violence that makes and maintains the chattel-slave and, here's the rub, the dismally limited Western(ized) conception of freedom as "self-possession" takes all of this violence for granted. Thus, it is no coincidence that there are more people living as slaves today than ever before in human history, at least 50 million people.

There is nothing natural or necessary about a society in which persons are (self-)possessed. Indeed, ideals and practices of (self-)possession are absent from many non-Western(ized) cultures, and when they are present, such ideals and practices very often have a limited sphere of influence, being circumscribed by other ideals and practices that take precedence. In many, if not most, cultures prior to the global hegemony of the imperialist white-supremacist capitalist patriarchal West, everyday affairs have tended to be defined by what David Graeber calls "baseline communism":

[T]he understanding that, unless people consider themselves enemies, if the need is considered great enough, or the cost considered reasonable enough, the principle of "from each according to their abilities, to each according to their needs" will be assumed to apply... Almost everyone follows this principle if they are collaborating on some common project.

A "great need" could be the need to avert a deadly disaster, such as a child falling onto the subway tracks. A "reasonable cost" might be giving a cigarette, or not answering a request to "hand me that wrench" with, "What do I get out of it?"

Seeing the world through Graeber's lens, one finds that ideals and practices of (self-)possession can only ever take precedence and dominate social relations when and where such communistic relations break down and enmity prevails amongst peoples. What's more, wage-slavery and chattel-slavery, which are founded upon ideals and practices of (self-)possession, effectively propagate themselves by and through employing violence and threats of violence, ranging from the crude to the subtle, that encourage just such breakdowns, that encourage enmity and prevent the repair and (re-)creation of communistic relations amongst peoples.

Graeber writes that the "surest way to know that one is in the presence of communistic relations is that not only are no accounts taken, but it would be considered offensive, or simply bizarre, to even consider doing so." The reverse is equally true: the surest way to know that one is living through a breakdown of communistic relations and an increase of enmity amongst peoples is that there is an ever increasing demand for things to be measured and accounted for. To quote Graeber one last time:

[I]mpersonal rules and regulations...can only operate if they are backed up by the threat of force. And indeed, in this most recent phase of [financialization], we've seen security cameras, police scooters, issuers of temporary ID cards, and men and women in a variety of uniforms acting in either public or private capacities, trained in tactics of menacing, intimidating, and ultimately deploying physical violence, appear just about everywhere — even in places such as playgrounds, primary schools, college campuses, hospitals, libraries, parks, or beach resorts, where fifty years ago their presence would have been considered scandalous, or simply weird.

The fact that it is possible for people today to talk about the "financialization of everyday life" and the fact that "performance metrics" have been introduced into almost every sphere of life in our globalized and technologically networked society, are two clear indications that communistic relations are in trouble. It is no wonder, then, that we find institutions deploying violence and threats of violence everywhere.

PART II. (ANTI-)BLACKNESS

Thus far, I've treated wage-slavery and chattel-slavery as ahistorical abstractions. But I will now need to recognize the fact that the concrete forms of wage-slavery and chattel-slavery that we are living with today are intimately and inextricably interlocked with racism. To be specific, anti-Black racism. As Cedric Robinson wrote, anti-Black racism has been Euro-Atlantic capitalist imperialism's "epistemology, its ordering principle, its organizing structure, its moral authority, its economy of justice, commerce, and power."

Frank B. Wilderson III, in a interview titled "Blacks and the Master/Slave Relation", describes the fundamental thrust of this ugly truth succinctly, referring to two important historical milestones: 625, when the King of Islamised Egypt conquered a kingdom in the *bilād al-sūdān* (i.e., the "land of the blacks", now known as the Sudan) and imposed a treaty on the kingdom that demanded hundreds of slaves be supplied to the Muslim king of Egypt every year; and 1452, when the Catholic Church issued a papal bull that legally granted Portugal the right to enslave any and all people they encountered south of Cape Bojador, on the coast of Western Sahara:

[T]here is a global consensus that Africa is the location of sentient beings who are outside

of the global community, who are socially dead. That global consensus begins with the Arabs in 625, and was passed on to the Europeans in 1452. Prior to that global consensus you can't think Black. You can think Uganda, Ashanti, Ndebele, you can think many different cultural identities, but Blackness cannot be dis-imbricated from the global consensus that decides [Africa is the land of the socially dead].

Putting aside all that the Euro-Atlantic West plagiarized from the Islamic world, the notion that dark-skinned peoples from Africa constituted a biopolitical race of human beings known as Black/Negro who are, by nature, well-suited for slavery — as opposed to being infidels or *kafirs* disfavored by Allah but upon whom He may still bestow grace or *baraka* at any moment according to His will — was a specific Western social invention entailing a great deal more than just slavery and social death. As R.A. Judy writes in the book Sentient Flesh, the Euro-Atlantic version of the imposed designation "Black/Negro" has two distinct senses. On the one hand, the imposed designation has a biopolitical-economic sense: "the word Negro, along with all its cognates, entails an anthropological categorization, whereby those so designated belong to a physically distinct type of not fully human hominid, which is what makes them legitimately available as prospective commodity assets." On the other hand, the imposed designation "Negro" carries an ethnographic sense, "the term connotes not only the slave formed in capitalism but also the populations of people who may be enslaved, and who remain Negro after slavery's abolition."

The biopolitical-economic sense of the designation Black/Negro is thus the definitive sense: the ethnographic Black/Negro being nothing other than the person susceptible to becoming Black/Negro in the biopolitical-economic sense. Using myself as an example here, being a child of dark-complexioned persons from Sub-Saharan Africa, I am Black/Negro in the ethnographic sense, which is to say, in other words, that I am a person susceptible to receiving the biopolitical-economic designation Black/Negro under the power formation of racialized slavery. That my ancestors were not enslaved by the European settlers of the New World and that the power formation of racialized slavery is no longer explicitly operative today does not put an end to my being Black/Negro in the ethnographic sense: I continue to be ethnographically Black/Negro because the power formation of racialized slavery did explicitly operate for a period of time, and the remnants of its explicit operation have been repurposed in the biopolitical-economic power formations that have succeeded those of racialized slavery.

Considering that chattel-slavery can only be maintained and advanced by violence and threats of violence that work to undermine communistic relations and promote enmity amongst peoples, imagine the almost unimaginable violence that was deployed to undermine communistic relations and to promote enmity amongst the peoples of Africa so as to effectively turn Africa into "a warren for the commercial hunting of black-skins. We often speak of the tens of millions of enslaved Africans who crossed the Atlantic. We often speak of the millions more enslaved Africans who died on the trek to the coast, and in captivity before ever boarding a slave ship. We do not speak enough of the millions of Africans who were never enslaved but were tortured and murdered to establish and maintain the social conditions that enabled their fellow Africans to be enslaved — that is to say, we speak too little of those brutalized in order to ruin communistic relations and generate a climate of enmity throughout Sub-Saharan Africa from the fifteenth century through the nineteenth century.

With that in mind let us now imagine the almost unimaginable violence that was deployed to institute, maintain, and advance racialized chattel-slavery in the New World. Such "scenes of subjection", as Saidiya Hartman would say, served to ruin possibilities for communistic relations with and amongst Black peoples, and to inspire widespread enmity towards Black peoples amongst peoples of all races. The brutality that undermined communistic relations with and amongst Black peoples in the New World was what legitimated the possession of blacks as chattel-slaves and established the "Negro race" as the "slave race". What needs to be stressed here is that such violence served to inspire enmity towards Black peoples amongst peoples of all races all over the world — not just amongst white European peoples, but also amongst the indigenous peoples of the New World, the peoples of South and East Asia, the peoples of the Middle East, and, perhaps most importantly, the Black peoples of Africa themselves. Such enmity persists to this day. The world continues to reject the communistic principle "from each according to his ability, to each according to their needs" with (dis)respect to Black peoples, such that Black peoples are regularly tasked with doing far more than anyone is able to do, while also being given far less than what they need to survive and thrive.

Why go to such outrageous extremes of violence, when such extremes were not easy to perpetrate and perpetuate? The fact of the matter is this: the production of Negro chattel-slaves between the fifteenth and nineteenth centuries was the libidinal economic condition of possibility for the production of wage-slaves during that same period. The Europeans' ideals and practices that defined freedom as self-possession would not have made any libidinal economic sense without the making of the Negro chattel-slave. Freedom as self-possession can only become something to aspire to when one has to confront the possibility of being possessed by another. This is to say that it is only in relation to the chattel-slave that the wage-slave appears as a "free laborer" or "worker" to themself, and to the world at large.

At the same time it is imperative that self-possessed wage-slaves do not consider themselves kin to chattel-slaves possessed by slave-masters, lest the two conspire together to put an end to their respective slaveries. The corporal and symbolic violence that simultaneously produced the Negro race as slave race and the white wage-slave as free laborer effectively served to ensure that there was minimal kinship between wage-slaves and chattel slaves. In particular, the brutality that underscored taboos and laws against miscegenation — working by and through augmenting the white male patriarch's powers to intervene in and regulate the sexual intimacies and reproductive choices of the women of their household dominions — effectively served to progressively separate whites and other non-Black races from the Black race, preventing whites and other non-Black wage-slaves from forming kinship bonds with Black chattel-slaves. This is to say, in other words, that capitalism and patriarchy worked together, hand-in-hand, to invent the Black race as the slave race par excellence and, thereby, to create the conditions for the wage-slave to appear as a "free laborer".

Now, I imagine that some of you are thinking to yourselves, "Thankfully, chattel-slavery has been made illegal." I beseech you here, "Yes, but not so fast!" To borrow a phrase from Saidiya Hartman, emancipation in the United Settler States, and just about everywhere else, was in many senses a "non-event". The effective result of emancipation was, almost everywhere, the formation of an apartheid regime. In the United Settler States, although individual blacks were no longer owned by individual whites following emancipation, the Jim Crow laws (a.k.a., Amerikkkan apartheid) effectively maintained and reinforced the rights of whites as a social category (as the master race) to exercise *abusus* rights with respect to blacks as a social category (as the slave race). This means, in other words, that emancipation allowed individual blacks to claim self-possession, while Jim Crow effectively dispossessed blacks as a social category. There were no longer to be individual slaves, but there remained the "Negro race", which as a social category remained socially dead, slave-stock. Lynchings in the post-bellum United Settler States, which took off after emancipation and which were often executed as punishment for imagined attempts at miscegenatory sexual trespass, were spectacular demonstrations of the fact that, under Amerikkkan apartheid, whites as a social category could exercise *abusus* rights with (dis)respect to blacks as a social category in the name of protecting the purity of the (master) race with relative impunity and extreme prejudice — whiteness being deemed a shared possession or property of the master race that could be devalued by any white person being found in proximity to or intimate relations with a person of the black/slave race.

Hartman describes this failure of Reconstruction following emancipation in the United Settler States, and along with this failure, doubts about the claims of progress and the definition of freedom:

While the inferiority of blacks was no longer the legal standard, the various strategies of state racism produced a subjugated and subordinated class within the body politic, albeit in a neutral or egalitarian guise. Notwithstanding the negatory power of the Thirteenth Amendment, racial slavery was transformed rather than annulled. [...] [T]his transformation was manifested in debt-peonage and other forms of involuntary servitude that conscripted the newly emancipated and putative free laborer, an abiding legacy of Black inferiority and subjugation, and the regulatory power of a racist state obsessed with blood, sex, and procreation.

[...] In the aftermath of emancipation, miscegenation acquired a political currency that was perhaps unprecedented. During Reconstruction, states passed stricter antimiscegenation statutes. [...] This fixation on imagined sexual trespasses revealed the degree to which the integrity and security of whiteness depended upon Black subjugation. The commingling of the races as putative equals within the body politic threatened the integrity of both races — the mongrelization of the white race and/or the engulfment of freed blacks by the white race due to Saxon superiority. Thus the proximity and intimacy of Black and white bodies deemed proper or appropriate under the social relations of slavery became menacing in the aftermath of emancipation. [...] The production of a miscegenation crisis facilitated the classification and control of blacks as a subjugated population.

As individual Black slaves were granted the freedom of self-possession, more emphasis was placed on apartheid measures: the filtering and channeling of the Black race (as the slave race) apart from the white race (as master race) by increasingly elaborate codes of conduct. If individuals assigned to the Black race failed to conduct themselves properly, they could be lynched — subjected to *abusus* by any member of the white race — in order to prevent contagion and the defilement of the master race by the slave race.

Now, I imagine that some of you are now thinking, "Thankfully, the victories of the civil rights era put an end to the Jim Crow regime." "Yes, but not so fast!" Michelle Alexander and others have (in)famously written about a New Jim Crow (a.k.a., New Amerikkkan apartheid) that has developed from the Old Jim Crow, undermining the advances of the civil rights movement. Those advances codified laws, rights, and regulations that effectively outlawed lynchings and other extra-judicial practices wherein and whereby whites acting as private citizens belonging to the master race could exercise *abusus* rights over and against members of the Black slave race in order to protect purity as property of the master race. But what whites can no longer do as private citizens, they remain empowered to do either if they become public officials, or are deputized by public officials to act in the name of public health, public safety, and public order, with the term "public" effectively connoting the white race. The Black race no longer being the race of slaves par excellence but, instead, the race of criminals, delinquents, and underachievers par excellence.

Thus, following the civil rights movement, mass incarceration took off: there was a significant increase in the exercise of *abusus* rights against blacks being justified as a "public service" by police officers, prison wardens, public prosecutors, child welfare service providers, judges, other law enforcement officials, as well as those deputized (*a priori* or *ex post facto*) by such law enforcement officials. Today, blacks as a social category become chattel by being placed under arrest, institutionalized, or otherwise made into "wards of the state". The (deputized) public official is authorized to exercise *abusus* rights over Black "wards of the state" as long as they are able to cast their exercise of abusus rights as a public service, without any explicit reference to the existence of a "slave race", but instead with reference to a statistical population having a greater likelihood to exhibit criminal or delinquent behaviors. In practice, this has meant that anyone and everyone can, by proxy, potentially exercise *abusus* rights with (dis)respect to blacks as a social category by "snitching" and reporting Black persons to the police or another civil administrative agency, as public nuisances, public health threats, or public safety threats.

Emancipation and civil rights both turned on the dismally limited Western conception of freedom as self-possession, and the violence that such a conception of freedom takes for granted. There is undoubtedly a degree of salvation to be found in emancipation, which has kept individual white masters from legally owning and abusing individual Black slaves, and a degree of salvation to be found in civil and human rights, which has kept whites as private citizens from citing the need to prevent defilement of the white master race by the Black slave race in order to justify their abuses of Black people. But let us not overlook the fact that emancipation and civil rights have their limits. These limits are rendered cruelly apparent to us by and through the effects of the reigning paradigm of policing. In a profound text titled "The Avant-Garde of White-Supremacy", Steve

Martinot and Jared Sexton deftly articulate the post-civil rights era refiguration of chattel-slavery by way of this paradigm:

[The police] prowl, categorizing and profiling, often turning those profiles into murderous violence without (serious) fear of being called to account, all the while claiming impunity. What jars the imagination is not the fact of impunity itself, but the realization that they are simply people working a job, a job they secured by making an application at the personnel office. In events such as the shooting of Amadou Diallo, the true excessiveness is not in the massiveness of the shooting, but in the fact that these cops were there on the street looking for this event in the first place, as a matter of routine business. This spectacular evil is encased in a more inarticulable evil of banality, namely, that the state assigns certain individuals to (well-paying) jobs as hunters of human beings, a furtive protocol for which this shooting is simply the effect.

But they do more than prowl. They make problematic the whole notion of social responsibility such that we no longer know if the police are responsible to the judiciary and local administration or if the city is actually responsible to them, duty bound by impunity itself. [...] While the police wreak havoc on the lives of those they assault, exercising a license implicit in and extending racial profiling, they engage in a vital cultural labor. On the one hand, racial profiling enables those unprofiled (the average white man and white women who are linked to one) to ignore the experience of social dislocation that profiling produces. They may recognize the fact of profiling itself, but they are free from the feeling of dread. Indeed, profiling creates insouciance in an atmosphere of organized violence. Official discourse seeks to accustom us to thinking about state violence as a warranted part of the social order. For them the security of belonging accompanies the re-racialization of whiteness as the intensification of anti-blackness. The police elaborate the grounds for the extension of a renewed and reconfigured white supremacist political economic order. On the other hand, there is terror and the police are its vanguard. [...] One cannot master [this terror], regardless of the intimacy or longevity of one's experience with it. One can only sense its frightening closeness as a probability, as serial states of brutality or derogation. The dread and suffering of those in the way of these repeated spasms of violence is always here and always on the horizon.

Going further and digging deeper, we need to recognize that all of the above speaks to a reality beyond the refiguration of chattel-slavery through the paradigm of policing within one particular New World slave state. For what are the "humanitarian intervention" and the "development aid project" if not the exemplars of the paradigm of policing writ large on the world stage?

The ignorability of police and civil administrative impunity within the United Settler States has its counterpart in the ignorability of the impunity of the international peacekeeping forces and the philanthropic organizations that conduct "humanitarian interventions" and "development aid projects" in the "outlaw states" and "burdened societies" of Africa — with Africa being home to 34 of the 50 poorest states, many of whom are, effectively, "wards" of the administrative organs of the "international public". Similar to how police and civil administrative impunity in the United Settler States effectively serves to maintain the Black race as the slave race by another name, as the "criminal" or "delinquent" race, the impunity of the peacekeeping forces and the philanthropic organizations participating in "humanitarian interventions" and "development aid projects" in Africa effectively serves to maintain Africa as the land of the socially dead by another name, the dark continent of "failed" and "fragile" states.

What's more, many Black Africans today, fleeing extreme poverty in their homelands, undertake perilous journeys to wealthier, whiter nations, where police and civil administrations are licensed to profile them as "illegal immigrants" and to exercise *abusus* rights over and against them as a public service in the name of immigration and customs enforcement.

All of this forms the basis for a global apartheid that turns on "pass laws" that distinguish between whites, blacks, and coloreds by using nationality as a proxy for race. Today's ever more bureaucratized and militarized border regimes effectively serve to maintain the privileges of those who have citizenship or legal residency in the wealthier, whiter nations of Empire — the caveat being that a greater degree of global mobility is granted to a select few from the poorer colored and Black nations of the periphery who are considered to be good prospects for facilitating outflows of financial, human, and natural resources from the poorer Black and colored periphery to the wealthier, whiter core, where so much ill-gotten wealth is being amassed and enjoyed.

Those whose nationalities are approximate blackness endure the worst and most discriminatory treatment under these bureaucratized and militarized border regimes. Police, judicial, and penal practices in all of the wealthier, whiter core nations of Empire converge in that they are applied with special diligence and severity to persons of non-white phenotypes, who are easily spotted and made to bend to the police and the judiciary, to the point that one may speak of a veritable process of criminalization of "immigrants" in general, and of Black immigrants in particular, with Black peoples being the first to be spotted for having been cast as the exemplars of the non-white phenotype.

PART III. ABOLITION

Against the "burdened individuality" of freedom as self-possession, abolitionists today are striving to realize communistic ideals and practices of freedom — that is, freedom from any and all forms of violence that would force people to give more than they are able, while being given less than what they need. To put a positive spin on it, abolitionists today are striving to (re-)construct a world in which everyone is free to give no more than they are able to give, and to receive as much as they need to live and thrive — a world in which there are no chattel-slaves, no slave-masters, no wage-slaves, and no capitalists.

To function as a chattel-slave is to be dispossessed of one's person, denied what one needs in order to live and thrive, and forced to endure injury by having to do more than one is able.

To function as a slave-master is to possess and exercise *abusus* rights over chattel-slaves; it is to have the freedom to demand that the chattel-slave do injury to themself by doing more than they are able, and to have the freedom to deny the chattel-slave what they need in order to live and thrive.

To function as a self-possessed wage-slave (or a so-called "free laborer" or "worker") is to have the freedom to do injury to oneself by demanding more of oneself than one is able and, in addition, to have the freedom to deny oneself what one needs in order to live and thrive. The self-possessed wage-slave is not, in fact, free to give no more than they are able and to receive as much as they need. Rather, to the contrary, the wage-slave is only free to exploit themself unto sickness and death. Given that the wage-slave must sell their *usus* and *fructus* rights to others in order to earn a living, all that the wage-slave retains for themself is their *abusus* rights. Ay, and here's the rub, the wage-slave struggling to make a living is often forced to exercise their *abusus* rights over their own person by obligating themself to do more than what they are able and to receive less than what they need.

To function as a capitalist is to be self-possessed but, instead of being forced to make a living by selling your *usus* and *fructus* rights to others, the capitalist makes a living buying others' *usus* and *fructus* rights and by investing in and lending money to other capitalists, slave-masters, and underpaid or unemployed wage-slaves. The capitalist only ever exercises their *abusus* rights over their own person in order to demonstrate and enjoy freedom as self-possession as a privilege, unlike the wage-slave who must do so in order to make a living.

The capitalist/wage-slave relation cannot be disentangled from the slave-master/chattel-slave relation, for the latter is the libidinal economic condition of possibility for the former. The existence of the slave-master/chattel-slave relation is what makes it possible for us to conceive of and desire freedom as self-possession and, thus, to conceive of and desire the capitalist/wage-slave relation as one we can enter into freely.

Going further and digging deeper, the specific slave-master/chattel-slave relations that condition capitalist/wage-slave relations today, in our deathly world of suffering, are entangled with anti-Black racism. The formations of bio-political-economy during modernity were such that Black peoples were *de jure* and *de facto* the premiere chattel-slaves between the 16th century and the 19th century. Ay, and following the "non-events" of emancipation, decolonization, civil rights and human rights legislation, we find that, today, an anti-Black paradigm of policing, writ large in the form of a global apartheid regime, has refigured the former slave race as the criminal and delinquent race and refigured the ancestral homelands of the former slave race as outlaw and burdened states. Police and other civil administrators, intra-nationally and inter-nationally, are employed to prowl, categorize and profile Black people as delinquents, strip them of their autonomy, and to make them into "wards" of public institutions.

The social roles of the chattel-slave, the slave-master, the wage-slave, and the capitalist are today upheld by the existence of police and the prisons that the police are tasked with filling. It is no wonder that the Tiqqun collective writes in its "Preliminaries to any Struggle against Prisons",

The function of prison in the overall economy of servitude is to materialize the false distinction between criminals and non-criminals, between law-abiding citizens and delinquents. This "purpose" is as much social as it is psychic. It is the imprisonment and torture of the prisoner that produces the citizen's feeling of innocence. Thus, as long as the criminal aspect of all existence under Empire is not acknowledged, the need to punish and to see punished will persist, and every argument against prison will continue to miss the mark.

What needs to be added is this: Any and every argument against prison will continue to miss the mark if it doesn't also recognize that Black peoples are everywhere distinguished as the criminal and delinquent race par excellence for having first been brought into being by Western social invention as the slave race par excellence. Ay, and the exemplary "global citizen" is the rich white man for having been brought into being by the very same artifice as the exemplary slave master and capitalist. It is not just the imprisonment and torture of delinquents in general, but of Black delinquents in particular, anywhere and everywhere they are to be found across the globe, that produces the global citizen's feeling of innocence and, even more importantly, a willingness to accept the dismally limited Western conception of freedom as self-possession.

No wonder that the slogans Black Lives Matter and All Cops Are Bastards appeal globally to radicals struggling to realize communistic ideals and practices of freedom. Given the genesis and structure of our world, to struggle for communistic ideals and practices of freedom is to struggle for the abolition of (self-)possession; to struggle for the abolition of (self-)possession is to struggle for the abolition of anti-Black racism; and to struggle for the abolition of anti-Black racism is to struggle for the abolition of policing and prisons.

"TOWARD A GLOBAL IDEA OF RACE"

Over the course of the twentieth century, anti-colonial and anti-racist movements have bested the forces of liberal globalism in a war of position that has forced liberal globalists to repudiate white supremacy in theory, though not in practice.

Prior to the second World War, white supremacy was well regarded in the United Settler States and throughout the Euro-Atlantic West as the intended outcome and crowning achievement of liberal globalism. But in the wake of the successes of anti-colonial and anti-racist movements following the second World War, white supremacy has come to be poorly regarded as an unintended byproduct of liberal globalism, and liberal globalists today find themselves at great pains to maintain their distance from white supremacy and white supremacists.

Repudiations and distantiations aside, white supremacy remains an effect of liberal globalist myths and strategies of intervention. Like their eighteenth and nineteenth century predecessors, the liberal globalists of the twentieth and twenty-first centuries maintain that white supremacy is the unavoidable consequence of "progress" — citing books like *Guns, Germs, and Steel* by Jared Diamond and *Sapiens* by Yuval Noah Harari and abusing the concept of "path dependence" to this end. The primary difference is that twentieth and twenty-first century liberal globalists endeavor to put "harm reduction" measures (e.g., "affirmative action" and "diversity, equity, and inclusion" measures) in place to mitigate white supremacy because it is considered an unfortunate side-effect of liberal globalism's ministrations.

The founding myth of white supremacy and its guiding strategy of intervention was well articulated by Kurtz in Joseph Conrad's 1899 novella *Heart of Darkness* — "Exterminate all the brutes." The white supremacist believes that, either by God's grace or natural selection, the white race has emerged as the most civilized race and all other races of peoples are destined to either (i) serve the white race or (ii) face extermination at the hands of the white race for being found unfit to serve. According to this logic, the destiny of the white race is to colonize the world, to conquer all other races of peoples, to evaluate whether or not colonized peoples are fit to serve the white race, to put those found fit to work in their service, and to exterminate all the brutes that aren't fit to serve. The world historical exemplar of a white supremacist project was the pre-Civil War project of the United Settler States of Amerikkka writ large, which turned upon the enslavement of black-skins and the extermination of red-skins by white-skins.

The founding myth of liberal globalist racism, and its guiding strategy of intervention, serve as the conditions of possibility for white supremacy. In its most exemplary form, at least since its turn away from explicitly championing white supremacy, the liberal globalist myth and strategy of intervention was best articulated by Amerikkkaner sociologists from the University of Chicago who, during the early 20th century, came up with the theory of the "race relations cycle" — which proceeds from "conflict and competition," to "accommodation," to "assimilation," and, finally, to "amalgamation" or miscegenation — which, "is apparently progressive and irreversible." Generalizing from the Amerikkkaner experience of waves of migrations of different racialized white peoples of Europe, Amerikkkaner sociologists proposed that when peoples of different races first come into contact, they inevitably enter into conflict with one another over their cultural differences and compete with one another for resources. After a period of conflict and competition that can be more or less prolonged, peoples of different races will eventually learn to accommodate each others' differences and to share resources. During this period of accommodation, peoples of different races inevitably become increasingly more familiar with each others' cultures and evaluate their cultural advantages and disadvantages. The races whose cultures are "primitive" will, slowly but surely, assimilate the better parts of the "more civilized" cultures of other races, having recognized the advantages of adopting the more civilized culture and the disadvantages of holding fast to their more primitive culture. The assimilated will become desirable partners for peoples of other races and they will themselves come to desire intimacies and children with peoples belonging to races with more civilized cultures. The miscegenated offspring of such interracial desires will, in their turn, physically blend in and likely tend towards forming intimacies and having children with persons belonging to races with more civilized cultures. Generation by generation, those races whose cultures are more primitive will be obliterated along with their more primitive cultures for failing to reproduce, and their remnants will be engulfed and absorbed into the more civilized race and their more civilized culture.

The "race relations cycle" is successfully completed when those belonging to primitive races and cultures yield to those belonging to more civilized races and cultures as a result of assimilation and then amalgamation/miscegenation. Yet, it is not the successful completion of the race relations cycle but, rather, its failure that drives liberal globalism. As Denise Ferreira da Silva writes in *Toward a Global Idea of Race*, "Though [the race relations cycle] explained the trajectory of certain immigrant groups, Southern and Eastern Europeans, other subjugated 'races and cultures,' Blacks and Asians, were understood to be neither 'assimilating' nor 'amalgamating' with the all-powerful [Northern and Western European] white race.

[...] The racial (physical) difference (via 'miscegenation') and cultural (moral/social) difference (via assimilation) of the others of [Northern and Western] Europe were supposed to naturally yield to the superior [Northern and Western European] race and culture, but stubborn persistence of [the] racial (physical) differences of Blacks and Asians prevented this." This is to say, in other words, that the race relations cycle runs into difficulties when it comes to blacks and Asians because the miscegenated offspring of white's liaisons with blacks and Asians are too physically (racially) different from the children of the more civilized white [Northern and Western] European race and, thus, fail to blend in with the white race. As a consequence, blacks and Asians are regarded to be physically (racially) undesirable partners for whites seeking to have children. Silva quotes the Amerikkkaner sociologist Robert E. Park's arguments to this effect.

"The chief obstacle to the assimilation of the Negro and the Oriental," Park argued, was "not mental but physical traits. It is not because the Negro and the Japanese are so differently constituted that they do not assimilate. If they are given an opportunity, the Japanese are quite as capable as the Italians, the Armenians, or the Slavs of acquiring our culture, and sharing our national ideals. The trouble is not with the Japanese mind but with the Japanese skin". Unlike Southern and Eastern [European] immigrants, Park argues, Asians and Blacks exhibit "physical traits," signs of "social (moral) distance," that do not disappear in the second generation. These marks entail reactions on the part of the "native" group, ideas and practices expressing prejudices, that exacerbate the "race conflict," preventing [their] "assimilation." That is, because they "fail" to lose the "visible" signs (racial difference) of cultural ("social/moral") difference, Blacks and Asians are the "strangers" whose presence transforms an otherwise transparent social configuration into one that is pathological — not ruled by universality and self-determination — one that fails to fulfill the logic of obliteration prescribed in the "theory of racial and cultural contacts."

Taught to fear this fate for their own children, Northern and Western Europeans will tend to refrain from miscegenation with Blacks and Asians, and Northern and Western European males in particular, granted their patriarchal privileges, will tend to refrain from producing "rightful heirs" via miscegenation with blacks and Asians.

A century following Park's sociological studies, however, things are changing with the shift of the global balance of power from the Euro-Atlantic to the Asia-Pacific. In accord with South African conventions from the Apartheid era, East Asians today are more and more often being counted as "honorary whites," rich enough to (almost) qualify as white — although it must be said that many white Europeans and Amerikkkans resent the bestowal of this "honor" on East Asians, a sentiment that has led to increasing anti-Asian racism and violence in the United Settler States. But whereas the overlap between East Asianness and whiteness is now in dispute, blackness and whiteness remain polar opposites. Blacks as a race are barred from becoming "honorary whites" due to the fact that the analytics of raciality are such that blackness has been deemed the opposite of whiteness, with whiteness meaning civilized and blackness meaning primitive/uncivilized. Only the most exceptional Black individuals are granted "honorary white" status, and these exceptional individuals are treated as if they have transcended the Black race, not as examples proving the Black race as a whole may be deserving of "honorary white" status.

Going further and digging deeper, liberal globalism effectively turns on the denigration of the so-called "race consciousness" of Black and other colored peoples who aren't able to pass for (honorary) whites. The so-called "race consciousness" of Black and colored peoples is their consciousness of being estranged from a white-dominant Northern and Western European culture because of their physical (racial) differences. According to the liberal globalist, "race consciousness" corrupts the Black and colored person's adoption of white culture in such a manner that effectively creates primitive racialized sub-cultures (e.g., African American culture) that mimic the more civilized cultures of white peoples but are retarded and warped by resentments that revolve around physical (racial) differences.

The problem for the liberal globalist, then, is what to do with Black and colored peoples relegated to primitive racialized subcultures. White supremacy is, in effect, a kind of "final solution." White supremacy seeks (i) to subordinate and compel into service those peoples of primitive racialized subcultures who are fit to serve the white race and its more civilized culture, and (ii) to exterminate those peoples of primitive racialized subcultures who are unfit to serve. In other words, liberal globalism is the set-up and white supremacy is the punchline: after liberal globalism has denigrated all those who are unfit for miscegenation as brutes, white supremacy proceeds to exterminate all the brutes who are unfit to serve the white race and its more civilized culture. Liberal globalists who repudiate white supremacy today are setting up the punchline but withholding on its delivery. They are repudiating the genocidal project of exterminating all the brutes, yes, but they are not repudiating the ethnocidal project of denigrating Black and colored peoples and relegating them to primitive racialized sub-cultures that "ape" and "corrupt" the more civilized cultures of white peoples.

Going further and digging even deeper, we may learn a great deal more about liberal globalist racism by examining how its project of denigration has operated in Brazil versus how it has operated in the United Settler States. As

Denise Ferreira da Silva writes in *Towards a Global Idea of Race*:

The celebrated "career" of Africans in Brazil was [...] to slowly but surely disappear under the inescapable force of a European desire as miscegenation eliminated racial difference and ensured that, after slavery, the Brazilian social space was ruled by universality. "The most obvious effect of miscegenation," [the Amerikkkaner sociologist Donald Pierson argued], "is to eliminate the physical differences between the races. In Bahia intermixture has now, for more than four hundred years, been breaking down physical barriers and reducing the visibility of blackness which in the United Settler States has produced a heightened "race consciousness".

Silva notes, however, that what we see in Brazil is not the total elimination of "race consciousness" but, rather, a "race consciousness" that thinks in terms of continuous gradations between different colors of people and between blackness and whiteness. In the United Settler States, by contrast, "race consciousness" relies upon discrete racial categories: Black, white, brown, red, yellow. The continuous nature of "race consciousness" in Brazil can be explained by the fact that Brazilian whites, rather than maintaining themselves as "pure" whites, maintain themselves as "alloyed" whites. In chemistry, an alloyed metal retains properties of the pure metal that it contains, such as electrical conductivity, ductility, opacity, and luster, but has supplementary properties that the pure metal lacks, such as increased strength or hardness. Similarly, the "alloyed whites" of Brazil maintain that they have tempered their lineages with that of the indigene and the Black in order to strengthen and harden themselves to thrive in the tropics while still retaining the properties that pure whites possess.

The logic of obliteration through assimilation and miscegenation still reigns supreme for Brazilian racists but, unlike the Amerikkkan racists who believe that the logic of obliteration demands the progressive purification of Black and colored peoples into white people's over the course of generations, the Brazilian racist believes that the logic of obliteration demands the alloying of whiteness with blackness and coloredness over the course of generations to better enable whiteness to withstand life in the tropics. In other words, Brazilian racists believe that one gains value by physically appearing to possess a modest quantum of non-white ancestry; Amerikkkan racists, by contrast, believe one loses value by physically appearing to possess any quantum of non-white ancestry.

It would be wrong, however, to believe that there is a conflict between the Amerikkkan and Brazilian racists. Rather to the contrary, Amerikkkan racists understand and recognize the logic of Brazilian racists: they understand that it is the more temperate climate of the United Settler States that enables Amerikkkaners to place more value on "pure" whiteness and it is the tropical climate of Brazil that forces Brazilian whites to place more value on "alloyed" whiteness. This is an important point made in Silva's *Towards a Global Idea of Race*: the eschatology of obliteration through assimilation and miscegenation is supplemented by a global logic according to which climate and geography determine the degree to which whiteness is to be purified or alloyed.

Pure whiteness is a privilege that is only available to those who live in climates and geographies that are similar to those of Europe (e.g., North America); alloyed whiteness is a consolation for those who live in climates and geographies that differ from those of Europe but aren't considered inhospitable to white European settlement and dominance (e.g., South America); and primitive racialized sub-cultures that "ape" and "corrupt" the white-dominant global culture will prevail in places that are considered inhospitable to white European settlement and dominance (e.g., Central Africa).

In light of all of this, let me come to the most crucial point. No matter how strident its repudiations of white supremacy are, the liberal globalist project continues to grant pure whites and alloyed whites the power to incarcerate and execute any Black and colored persons who violently rebel against the white-dominant global culture, selectively but effectively reviving the white supremacist project of extermination and assigning it a limited policing function. This is to say that the liberal globalist who repudiates white supremacy is in reality doing no more than telling Black and colored peoples that they will not be subject to extermination in the manner advocated by white supremacists provided that they accept their denigration and resign themselves to a primitive racialized sub-culture that "apes" and "corrupts" the more civilized cultures of white peoples. Whether or not they are found fit to serve and are put to work, Black and colored peoples who accept their denigration are invited to petition liberal globalists for some rights and protections against the selective but effective revival of the white supremacist project of extermination as a policing project, but Black and colored peoples who resist and refuse denigration do so at their own peril.

Anti-colonial and antiracist movements, having forced liberal globalists to repudiate white supremacy, are now engaged in a new war of position to force liberal globalists to repudiate the myth that non-white peoples, the others of Europe, ought to disavow their primitive cultures and, instead, "ape" the more civilized cultures of white European peoples. This means pointing out that non-white peoples could only ever have been regarded as inferior to white Europeans in one crucial respect: "they lacked the European technology and culture of war, and were appalled by the all-destructive fury of European warfare." Though it is tempting for anti-racists and anti-colonialists to make the argument that the all-destructive fury of European warfare is evidence of the inferiority of white European culture, we must resist this temptation. For anti-racists and anti-colonialists to rank cultures according to their relative inferiority and superiority in any regard whatsoever is to concede significant ground to the liberal globalists in their war of position, given that there is no way to prove the superiority of one culture over another without assuming some form of colonization.

Anti-colonial and anti-racist movements against liberal globalism must (re) create myths and guiding strategies of contravention that obviate any need and desire to prove the superiority of one culture over another. They must, instead, facilitate correspondences and confluences amongst peoples of different cultures. They must enable increasingly diverse peoples to reciprocally defer to one another and blur and traverse the lines and boundaries between them despite continuing to differ from one another in profound ways, physically and otherwise. Liberal globalist initiatives cast differences, especially physical (racial) differences, as barriers for non-white individuals to overcome as they seek to be included in the white-dominant global culture. Opposed to the idea that we ought to "overcome our differences," anti-colonialist and anti-racist projects are all about creating ways for all of us to take pleasure and enjoyment in the creolizing play and variation of our differences.

WHITE
AMERIKKKANERS

Conversing and corresponding with readers of my earlier works, especially readers of my *Triptych* and *Other Related Matters*, I have noticed many of them de-contextualizing and de-historicizing my work, willfully ignoring the apocalyptic events that have shaped our world and, in turn, informed my work. Unsurprisingly, most of the readers who have maintained such willful ignorance to context and history have happened to be white Amerikkkaners — though it should be noted that white Europeans come a very close second in this regard.

Anyone who is surprised by white Amerikkkaners' disregard for such context and history need only remind themself that white Amerikkkaners are, statistically speaking, the most privileged people on our planet today. Despite only forming ~3% of the human population, white Amerikkkaners form more than 30% of the richest 1% of persons on our planet, with more white Amerikkkaners belonging to the richest ~1% than to the poorest ~50%, 1 in 7 relative to 1 in 12. To put white Amerikkkaner privilege in its proper context, note that China, with ~18% of the global population, has ~10% of the richest ~1%; India, with another ~18%, has ~1% of the richest ~1%; another ~18% of the global population is on the African continent but not even a thousandth of a percent of the richest ~1% are there.

There is no making sense of white Amerikkkaner privilege, as expressed by the startling statistics above, without cataloging the apocalyptic events that gave rise to the world in which white Amerikkkaners enjoy that privilege, events that shame and disturb most white Amerikkkaners so much that few can bear to think about them. Between the sixteenth and nineteenth century, a conservative estimate is that 100 million Natives died in the process of Euro-Atlantic capitalist imperialism being established. During the same time period, the conservative estimate is that 25 million Africans were kidnapped and subjected to the social death that is slavery, with millions more of their descendants born and bred to be slaves by Euro-Atlantic capitalist empires. Meanwhile, on the African continent, tens of millions more were murdered, first to facilitate the slave trade and then to bring raw materials to world markets dominated by the Euro-Atlantic capitalist empires. Further afield, tens of millions in India, China, and elsewhere in Asia died during famines and wars as their peoples were being forcibly incorporated as subordinates into political-economic structures dominated by the Euro-Atlantic capitalist empires, including tens of millions of Indians starved to grow opium that was pushed on the peoples of China at murderous European gunpoint. This catalog of horrors is not exhaustive. For one thing, I have only dealt with the human death tolls, disregarding the outrageous tolls on non-human others and the lasting tolls on the human psyche across the generations.

Dare you say that all of the above is a catalog of ancient history, it is estimated that 16 million people have died needlessly from malnutrition since 1990, during my own lifetime, due to policies conceived of by the bankers and bureaucrats of the so-called Washington Consensus and imposed upon poorer nations. These 16 million deaths could have been prevented with simple systems to ensure universal access to nutritious food. What's more, many of these neoliberal policies are still being pushed onto poorer, darker nations by richer, whiter nations today, despite the fact that climate catastrophes are wreaking havoc on poorer nations' lifeways, lands, and food supplies.

Going further and digging deeper, making sense of white Amerikkkaner privilege means making sense of the significant role that the United Settler States of Amerikkka played in the production of so many horrors since its inception in 1776. Let me briefly outline this history for those who require a refresher.

The United Settler States was founded as a racial capitalist slave empire, the effective result of a counter-revolution of white nationalist slavers and genocidal murderers against blacks and Natives who had begun to win concessions from the British Empire.

A century later, following emancipation and the "closing of the frontier", the United Settler States was transformed from a slave empire to an apartheid state, with its racial capitalist regime having come to turn on anti-Black segregation laws (i.e., Jim Crow), racist immigration laws (e.g., the Chinese Exclusion Act), and the concentration of Natives in reservations (the ideological precursors to the Nazi ghettos and concentration camps in Eastern Europe as well as the South African Bantustans).

Another century later, ignoring the persistence of the apartheid regime constituted by Native reservations, it could be said that the victories of the Civil Rights movement abolished the *de jure* apartheid regime only to have it replaced with the *de facto* apartheid regime that remains in place today. Black incomes on average are about 60 percent of white incomes, Black wealth on average is 5 to 7 percent of white wealth, many low and middle income blacks live in predominantly Black neighborhoods that lack the public amenities and public services that predominantly white and middle income neighborhoods enjoy, blacks are incarcerated in state prisons at nearly 5 times the rate of whites, one in 10 Black men are denied the right to vote for having committed a "crime," and the list goes on. That being said, the nation's transition from a *de jure* to a *de facto* apartheid regime has enabled a "talented tenth" of the Black population and other non-white populations — a set composed of persons who have had to over-achieve relative to their white peers and act as apologists for Amerikkkan imperialism and racism — to live as "honorary whites," enjoying access to offices and privileges that were previously reserved for whites only. This assumption of formerly white offices and privileges by non-whites, facilitated to a degree by "affirmative action" and "diversity and inclusion" programs, has provoked the ire of white nationalists, conservative media, and others seeking to "Make Amerikkka Great Again."

Shifting our focus from the intra-national to the inter-national arena, the United Settlers effectively used the excess wealth that they extracted from native lands and laborers of color to become the undisputed hegemon of the racial capitalist "modern world system" originally centered in Western Europe. This has been the case for nearly a century now, the United Settlers having capitalized on the decline of the British Empire over the course of the intra-imperialist World Wars (1914-1945), and the successive waves of anti-colonial struggles that followed in their wake. The list of countries targeted by the United Settler military since the nation's inception includes the vast majority of the nations on Earth, including almost every single country in Latin America and the Caribbean, and most of the African continent.

Using the so-called "Cold War" (1947-1991) with the Union of Soviet Socialist Republics as its initial cover, the United Settlers organized under their sponsorship and protection a global neocolonial system of client states, often ruled by terror, and it has overseen the development of a global apartheid regime that turns on "pass laws" that effectively distinguish between whites, blacks, and coloreds, by deferring to nationality as a proxy for race.

To the incredulity and indignation of all who are aware of the basic facts of Amerikkkan history, the official line that the United Settlers have stridently maintained is that theirs is "a nation born of freedom" and "dedicated to furthering the cause of democracy and human rights throughout the world, though it has occasionally erred in the pursuit of this objective." The gap between the facts of Amerikkkan history and the noble origins, values, and intentions claimed by the United Settlers today is a yawning chasm that ideological institutions — the media, schools, and universities — have worked tirelessly to bridge by rewriting history and trivializing memory. These ideological institutions have not entirely succeeded in winning their war of position against history and memory, but their accomplishments have been profound. Even amongst college educated white Amerikkkaners today, few know enough and fewer are brave enough to publicly and honestly speak of and to the most basic facts regarding the origins, development, and present realities of Amerikkkan imperialism and racism.

The history of Amerikkkan racism and imperialism is appalling: the horrors of the Third Reich, unspeakable as they are, pale in comparison. Admittedly, the United Settler States has had the advantage of time and staying power over the Third Reich, but that fact doesn't let the United Settlers off the hook. The majority of white Amerikkkaner adults are aware of this appalling history on a gut level, but many (if not most) white Amerikkkaners repress their awareness of this history and cover it up with wishful and defensive fantasies. Chief amongst the wishful fantasies is the one that I was taught in elementary and middle school in the 1990s, in which the United Settlers became the leaders of the "free world" by defeating the Third Reich and the Axis powers in World War II and then combating the spread of the communist menace issuing from the Soviet Union during the Cold War.

When confronting white Amerikkkaners with the context and history that informs their extreme privilege, the greatest difficulty I find is that many white Amerikkkaners refuse to differentiate power from privilege: they willfully misinterpret me to be telling them to abstain from enjoying the fruits of their privilege (their time and money) and, instead, to donate these fruits to the underprivileged. In fact, I am telling them to do something radical (from Latin *radix* "root"); I am telling them to counter the powers that form the roots of their privilege. Or, in other words, against that common sense phrase that has entered conventional wisdom, I am telling them, "Bite the hand that feeds you; this same hand is murdering our planet and the greater part of her peoples."

The devious ploys of "diversity, equity, and inclusion" (DEI) championed by liberal globalists in response to being confronted with context and history are, of course, designed to avoid attacking the roots of white Amerikkkaner privilege. DEI focuses on allocating a modest portion of the fruits of white Amerikkkaner privilege to the "talented tenths" that white dominant institutions fraction off from underprivileged non-white populations. This course of action has served to generate animus between the "talented tenths" and those less fortunate white Amerikkkaners aggrieved by such fruits being allocated to non-whites instead of other whites "in need" of them. This animus is not a flaw but a feature of the DEI push. The spectacle that liberal globalists have made of the animus between "talented tenths" and reactionary white Amerikkkaners draws our attention away from efforts to counter the powers that form the roots of white privilege.

I ask the following questions to privileged white Amerikkkaners who want to "do good" in the world:

Instead of allocating the fruits of your good schooling to underprivileged non-whites whose good grades place them in the "talented tenth," why not help us flee from schooling so that we might rebel against the school systems that degrade the larger part of the underprivileged non-white population and, in so doing, share our know-how otherwise?

Instead of allocating the fruits of your good finances to underprivileged non-whites whose good credit places them in the "talented tenth," why not help us flee from financing so that we might rebel against the financial systems that discredit the larger part of the underprivileged non-white population and, in so doing, share our resources otherwise?

Instead of allocating the fruits of your good timing to underprivileged non-whites whose timeliness places them in the "talented tenth," why not help us flee from calendaring and clocking so that we might rebel against the timing systems that delay the larger part of the underprivileged non-white population and, in so doing, share our time otherwise?

Instead of allocating the fruits of your high profile to underprivileged non-whites whose resumes, CVs, and other records of service place them in the "talented tenth," why not help us flee from profiling so that we might rebel against the (racial) profiling systems that demerit the larger part of the underprivileged non-white population and, in so doing, choose to share our life stories otherwise?

Western modernity's ideals and practices of freedom, which white Amerikkkaners have refined to a remarkable extreme, are ideals and practices of (self-)possession. When the white Amerikkkaner champions their own "freedom," they are championing their own self-possession with their left hand and the others' dispossession and captivity with their right hand. In other words, the white Amerikkkaner's freedom is not freedom from captivity but, to the contrary, it is the freedom to possess oneself while others are dispossessed of themselves and held captive. The white Amerikkkaner feels most free when demonstrating their own self-possession to those who are dispossessed, as when, for instance, the white Amerikkkaner chooses to donate their share of the fruits of white Amerikkkaner privilege (free time and money) to underprivileged non-whites. By contrast, white Amerikkkaners who participate in fugitive planning projects alongside nonwhites feel as if they are being dispossessed of themselves and, thus, losing their freedom. Thankfully, some white Amerikkkaners know themselves to be winning another kind of freedom in and through participating in our flights and rebellions: freedom from whiteness and the strangling restrictions that ideals and practices of (self-)possession place on friendship, love, community, and hospitality.

It is no wonder that statistics reveal a startling number of individual white Amerikkkaners to be in possession of assets worth a million dollars or more: the more assets that they possess, the freer most white Amerikkkaners feel themselves to be. Going further and digging deeper, the purification of Western modernity's ideals and practices of (self-)possession has been taken to such extremes by white Amerikkkaners that they now saturate most (if not all) aspects of white Amerikkkan life.

White Amerikkkaners are raised to treat their families, their friends, and their lovers like their possessions. The practical language of loving relationships amongst white Amerikkkaners is such that separated parents with joint custody over their children negotiate their parenting relationship like the ownership of a timeshare property; monogamous lovers negotiate their relationships with their romantic partners like enterprises over which one partner claims proprietor ownership or, alternatively, like joint-ventures under the dual ownership of the two partners; polyamorous lovers negotiate their multiple partnerships like diversified portfolios of shares; the person in search a romantic partner imagines themself to be "on the market"; and the breakup of a romantic relationship is negotiated in a manner akin to the liquidation of a corporation. Ay, the white Amerikkkaner who talks about "sharing" anything "equitably" is unlikely to be referring to the communal principle "from each according to their abilities, to each according to their needs," and most likely to be referring to the proportional distribution of ownership stakes to individuals joined in a social relationship imagined to be a form of enterprise, with little regard (if any at all) for peoples' differing needs and abilities.

I am the child of Black African immigrants from nations counted amongst the poorest on the planet. My parents came to the United Settler States seeking opportunities during the 1980s, around the time when white Amerikkkaners began issuing the following threat to the rest of the world: "It's morning again in Amerikkka." I have spent a good part of my life in the company of white Amerikkkaners and the "talented tenths" that excel at either emulating white Amerikkkaners or otherwise appealing to the white Amerikkkaner gaze. By the time I was ten years old, the imperative to become a Black man of distinction — a member of the "talented tenth" that apes, shucks, and jives for white Amerikkkaners — had been drummed into my ears, beamed into my eyes, and even beaten into my flesh. This is all to say, in other words, that everything that I have written about white Amerikkkaners here comes from learned experience, from a life thoroughly lived with what W.E.B. DuBois called a double-consciousness, "a sense of always looking at one's self through the eyes of [whites], of measuring one's soul by the tape of a [white] world that looks on in amused contempt and pity."

I offer you this personal background as a preface to an admission of bad conscience: I should have known better than to expect my white Amerikkkaner readers to recognize the context and history implicit in what I was writing. I already had every reason to believe that, if I wasn't explicit, my white Amerikkkaner readers would pretend as if the context and history that my writings assumed didn't exist. I knew very well that most of my white Amerikkkaner readers were unlikely to truly know any Black people who did not present to whites as aspirants to the distinction of belonging to the "talented tenth." Given that I was asking such white Amerikkkaner readers to read and support my work, it was imperative that I explicitly articulated the context and history that my writings assumed. My choice to ignore this imperative, to leave context and history implicit, was born of the reality that, not unlike my white Amerikkkaner readers, I too was afraid to bite the hand that feeds me. It ought to be said, however, that the traumatic experiences that taught me to be afraid were of a markedly different timbre from those of my white Amerikkkaner readers, especially given that our differing experiences should not be disentangled from those of our respective ancestors. What's more, having dropped out of the academic rat race, I could not count on the "scholastic sanctuary" accorded to radical Black scholars with proper credentials from white dominant institutions and license to contextualize and historicize while Black. Nevertheless, given that I invited white Amerikkkaner readers to the table, the imperative wasn't mine to ignore: context and history needed to be made explicit or they simply would not be for my white Amerikkkaner readers.

In writing this book I have dispatched with the fear and heeded the imperative: I have explicitly addressed context and history, again and again. Heeding the imperative by no means assures that my white Amerikkkaner readers will embrace context and history, but it assuredly makes ignoring context and history an active choice for them. This course of action has given me a liberating sense for which of my white Amerikkkaner readers are actually worth cultivating and, more profoundly still, it has given me a liberating sense for whether, when, and to what degree it is (un)important for me to cultivate white Amerikkkaner readers at all, for there are many other readers worth seeking and cultivating.

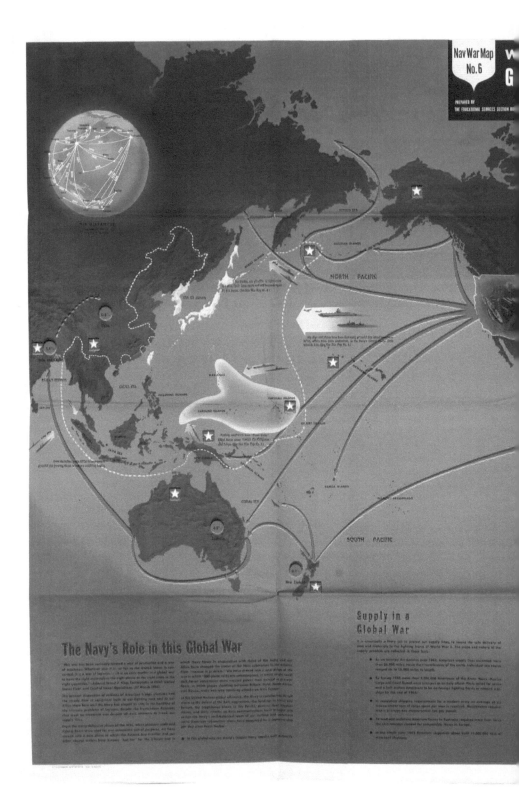

The Navy's Role in this Global War

Supply in a Global War

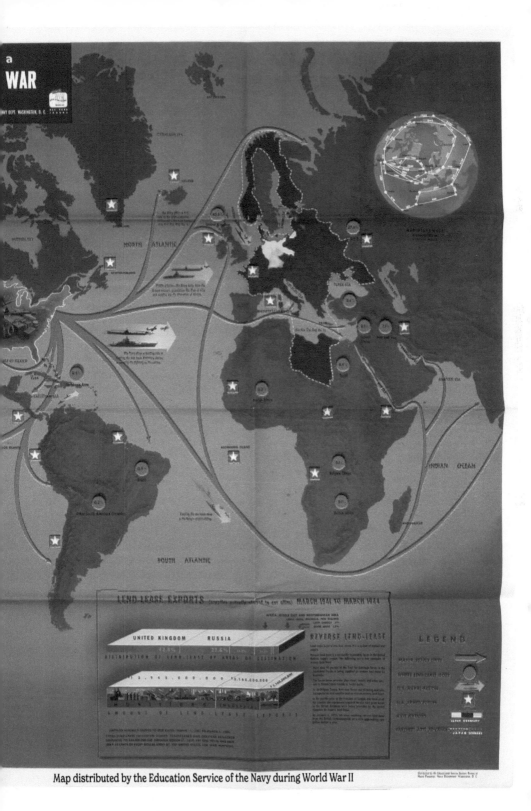

Map distributed by the Education Service of the Navy during World War II

THE
SHAPE
OF
THINGS
TO
COME

Giovanni Arrighi's *Long Twentieth Century* is the finest book that I have read on the dynamics of five centuries of capitalist imperialism. The book takes the reader on an epic journey through time: from the Long Sixteenth Century, the heyday of the Genoese-Iberian hegemony that laid the foundations for capitalist imperialism; to the Long Seventeenth Century, the heyday of the Dutch hegemony that brought the global capitalist joint-stock corporation into being; to the Long Nineteenth Century, the heyday of the British hegemony that transformed capitalist imperialism by and through doubling down on industrialization; and, finally, to the Long Twentieth Century itself, the heyday of the Amerikkkaner hegemony whose most unique characteristic was being more intentional about putting (capital "E") Empire above (little "e") empire, building international Imperial institutions (e.g., the International Monetary Fund, the World Bank, and the World Trade Organization) so that multi-national capitalist corporations could more effectively transform transaction costs from liabilities into assets .

The dynamics of capitalist imperialism described by Arrighi have been driven by capitalists' need to "internalize" costs that were previously "externalized" in order to resolve crises of over-accumulation. The term "internalize" can be a tad misleading, however, as capitalists do not simply absorb the costs that they "internalize." Rather, capitalists transform the costs that they "internalize" from liabilities to capital assets. Over-accumulation crises emerge whenever capitalists in possession of immense surpluses of money cannot find enough places to safely and profitably invest their surpluses. Over-accumulation crises are resolved when capitalists manage to find ways to safely and profitably invest their surpluses in enterprises that effectively transform externalities that were previously liabilities into capital assets.

The Genoese were cosmopolitan financial capitalists through and through — which is to say, in other words, that they externalized as many costs as they could: protection, production, transaction, and reproduction costs alike. The Genoese made their money by investing in the imperial enterprises of the Iberians (the Spanish and the Portuguese), receiving shares of the profits of successful imperial enterprises and earning fees and interest on debts owed to them no matter whether imperial enterprises succeeded or failed. Hence, the first period of capitalist imperialism, the Long Sixteenth Century, is known as the period of Genoese-Iberian hegemony: the Genoese were the capitalist hegemon, the Iberians were the imperialist hegemon, and the formation the Genoese-Iberian capitalist-imperialist alliance was, effectively, the founding act of capitalist imperialism.

The Dutch internalized the protection costs that the Genoese had externalized; in so doing, the Dutch transformed the means and relations of organizing protection for imperialist enterprises from liabilities into capital assets. Whereas the Genoese capitalists needed the Spanish and Portuguese aristocratic imperialists to protect the enterprises that they invested in; the Dutch East India Company, which was established in 1602 as the first joint stock company, was a capitalist imperialist enterprise that maintained military forces fully capable of protecting the enterprises that it invested in. This is to say, in other words, that the Genoese-Iberian alliance between capitalists and imperialists, as two separate factions, was overtaken by a unified faction of Dutch capitalist imperialists during the Long Seventeenth Century.

The British internalized the production costs that the Genoese and the Dutch had both externalized; in so doing, the British transformed the means and relations of organizing global production from liabilities into capital assets. Whereas the leading Dutch capitalist imperialists profited mostly from financing and protecting the movement of goods manufactured all around the globe, the leading British capitalist imperialists also profited from organizing the industrial manufacture of goods all around the globe. This is to say that industrialization enabled British capitalist imperialists to profit from lowering the material, labor, and logistics costs of global production in addition to profiting from financing and protecting global supply-chains. What's more, the leading British capitalist imperialists effectively established the imperialist nation-state as a protection services provider for capitalist imperialist enterprises, transforming the public financing of national debts into the financing of protection costs for capitalist-imperialist enterprises.

The United Settlers internalized the transaction costs that the Genoese, the Dutch and the British had all externalized; in so doing, the United Settlers transformed the means and relations of organizing global transactions from liabilities into capital assets. Whereas the leading British capitalist imperialists primarily profited from the industrial manufacture of goods and from financing and protecting global supply-chains, the leading Amerikkkaner capitalist imperialists profited just as much from the marketing of goods and complementary services around the globe. Marketing here includes "the selection of target markets; the selection of certain attributes or themes to emphasize in advertising; the operation of advertising campaigns; the design of products and packaging attractive to buyers; the definition of the terms of sale, such as prices, discounts, warranties, [consumer financing,] and return policies; the placement of products in media or with people believed to influence the buying habits of others; the negotiation of agreements with retailers, wholesale distributors, [franchisees,] and resellers; the organization of efforts to create awareness of, loyalty to, and positive feelings about a brand; etc." What's more, the leading Amerikkkaner capitalist imperialists also reimagined and reorganized the imperialist nation-state so that, in addition to being a provider of protection services, the imperialist nation-state also became a provider of social services that enabled and encouraged its subject populations to adopt a consumerist ideology and fit into a consumer society. The public financing of national debts under Amerikkkaner hegemony went beyond the financing of protection costs for capitalist imperialists, and included the financing of those transaction costs necessary for the maintenance of a consumer society that no individual imperialist capitalist enterprise could bear on its own.

After laying out the history summarized above, Arrighi's book goes on to suggest that, if capitalist imperialism is to survive the over-accumulation crises that are presently threatening it, capitalist imperialists will now need to find ways to internalize "reproduction costs" that they have previously treated as externalities. The term "reproduction costs" refers to the costs of sustaining cultural and natural resources, and contemporary capitalist imperialists' new found concern for "sustainable development" is primarily about transforming the costs of sustaining cultural and natural resources from liabilities into capital assets.

Lest you think that this new found capitalist concern for "sustainable development" bodes well for culture and nature, let me make something clear to you. Every capitalist endeavor to internalize costs previously considered externalities has, thus far, been an ethnocidal and ecocidal endeavor: the more costs capitalist imperialists internalize, the more capitalist imperialism takes hold of life and squeezes out those parts of life that do not yield any profits. If capitalist imperialists can successfully internalize the costs of sustaining cultural and natural resources, capitalist imperialists can refuse to sustain those aspects of culture and nature that do not yield profits for them and they can choose to sustain only those aspects that do yield profits for them.

Attempts to sustain that which is profitable about culture and nature will be celebrated as a "moral achievement" by capitalist imperialists given that, heretofore, capitalist imperialists had only ever exploited cultural and natural resources with little concern for sustaining these resources for future generations. Ay, but this "moral achievement" by capitalist imperialists will, in fact, be a cultural and natural catastrophe: promoting global Sustainable Development Goals that diminish all that is unprofitable about culture and nature effectively means promoting ethnocides and ecocides of an unprecedented scale and scope in order to privilege the proliferation of that which is profitable. The onus will be on marginal peoples and marginal places to demonstrate to capitalist imperialists that they possess cultural and natural resources worth sustaining, either because they present profitable ecosystem services or opportunities for "social entrepreneurship."

Going further and digging deeper, it is important to recognize that, historically, prevailing hegemons have found it difficult to resolve over-accumulation crises by internalizing externalities, while upstarts (i.e., "would-be hegemons") have found it easier to resolve over-accumulation crises. This is because the prevailing hegemons do not experience over-accumulation crises as acutely as upstarts do. Prevailing hegemons are usually so powerful that they cannot only weather over-accumulation crises but, more profoundly still, prevailing hegemons can actually take great pleasure in exercising their dominance over others during over-accumulation crises. In fact, this is precisely what hegemony is all about, and why it is sought after. Indeed, established hegemons have been known to aggravate over-accumulation crises in order to heighten the pleasure they take in dominating lesser powers during times of crisis. As a result, prevailing hegemons are unlikely to seize the initiative when it comes to resolving over-accumulation crises — that is, of course, not until prevailing hegemons observe upstarts effectively seizing the initiative and threatening to overtake them. By then, however, it is usually too late: the upstart who successfully seizes the initiative to resolve a crisis first, and who then effectively defends their seized initiative with military force, is usually able to demote the old hegemon and become the new hegemon.

During the transition from the Long Sixteenth to the Long Seventeenth Century, the Dutch seized the initiative from the Genoese by internalizing protection costs, and the Dutch successfully defended their seized initiative against the Genoese-Iberian alliance. That being said, however, the Dutch failed to defend their seized initiative against their allies in their wars against the Iberians, the British and the French. As Arrighi notes, "Dutch world hegemony was [...] a highly ephemeral formation." For most of the Long Seventeenth Century — from the outbreak of the Anglo-Dutch Wars in 1652 (a mere four years after the Settlement of Westphalia with the Iberians) to the end of the Napoleonic Wars in 1815 — the British and the French were locked in competition to become the hegemonic power who would take over from the dwindling Dutch.

During the transition from the Long Seventeenth to the Long Nineteenth Century, the British seized the initiative by internalizing production costs, and they successfully defended their seized initiative against the French during the Napoleonic Wars. The British, unlike the Dutch, effectively dominated their

Long Century, serving as the conductor and primary beneficiary of the "Concert of Europe".

During the transition from the Long Nineteenth to the Long Twentieth Century, the Amerikkkaners and the Germans both managed to seize the initiative in internalizing transaction costs. However, whereas the Germans had to confront British hegemony directly as they seized the initiative, the Amerikkkaners were able to ally themselves with the British against the Germans. The Amerikkkaners effectively demoted the British and became the new hegemon after the World Wars fought against Germany had effectively exhausted the British and empowered the Amerikkkaners vis-à-vis the British.

It is important to note that the Germans were forced to confront the British directly because the Germans, unlike the Amerikkkaners, did not have an expansive territorial empire from which they could extract resources. As they sought to seize the initiative, the Germans found that they had to build an expansive territorial empire by seizing territories from and upsetting other imperial powers, including the British. The Amerikkkaners, by contrast, didn't have to confront the British directly because the Amerikkkaners already possessed an expansive territorial empire. Arrighi quotes Gareth Stedman Jones on this point, "historians who speak complacently of the absence of the [imperialism] characteristic of European powers merely conceal the fact that the whole internal history of U.S. imperialism was one vast process of territorial seizure and occupation. The absence of territorialism 'abroad' was founded on an unprecedented territorialism 'at home.'"

During the Long Twentieth Century, the Amerikkaners successfully secured and defended their hegemony not only against rival capitalist powers but also against rival anti-capitalist powers. The Amerikkaners have fought and "won" three world wars during the rise and tenure of the United Settler States as hegemon — two hot wars (World Wars I and II against German capitalist imperialists and their allies) and one cold war (the Global Cold War against Soviet communist imperialists and their allies). In and through the process of fighting these three world wars, the Amerikkkaners have amassed outrageous stockpiles of weapons of mass destruction and they have organized the means and logistics needed to deploy weapons of mass destruction almost anywhere on the globe at any time. This means that the Amerikkkaners can effectively threaten to destroy all life on Earth in an all-consuming conflagration before ever giving up hegemony.

Today, as over-accumulation crises abound and threaten to undermine Amerikkkaner hegemony, it is very likely that an upstart power might seize the initiative when it comes to internalizing reproduction costs, but it is very unlikely that an upstart power will be able to defend its seized initiative against the Amerikkkaners without provoking a war that cannot be won. The Amerikkkaners recognize this and, instead of seizing the initiative first and going all in on sustainable development, the Amerikkkaners are doubling down on military spending, further ensuring that any upstart power that manages to seize the initiative will never be able to successfully defend its seized initiative against them.

The threat of nuclear war is one game-changer in the capitalist imperialist competition to achieve world hegemony. The climate crisis is another. Chances are that we are not living through a phase change from a relatively stable climate regime that is cooler to another relatively stable regime that is hotter but, rather, that we are living through a phase change from a relatively stable climate regime to a chaotic climate regime. All the predictive models of political economy, all of the normalizing and optimizing powers of capitalist imperialism, assume that a relatively stable climate regime can be maintained. If we are entering a chaotic climate regime, all of these models will no longer be able to effectively normalize and optimize the global economy any longer: over-accumulation crises will become much more frequent and much more acute as it becomes harder and harder for capitalist imperialists to manage risks by exercising normalizing and optimizing powers that render the global economy predictable. It follows from this that it will become harder and harder for the leading hegemon, the United Settler States, to weather over-accumulation crises and, perhaps, this may spur them to buck the historical trend and seize the initiative first when it comes to internalizing the costs of sustaining cultural and natural resources. Admittedly, this does not seem to be the case at present, but the climate catastrophes have only just begun...

Now, having summarized Arrighi's book, I must mention that there is one feature of Arrighi's book that feels to me like a major flaw. His book helps us make sense of the forces driving the actions of capitalist imperialists, yes, but it doesn't help us make sense of the forces driving the actions of anti-imperialists and anti-capitalists.

Arrighi's book invites the reader to ask the questions that the most discerning capitalist imperialists are presently asking themselves... Will the Amerikkkaners hold on to their hegemony at any cost, even if that means nuclear war? Will the People's Republic of China, the most powerful upstart power today, try to seize the initiative and make an aggressive bid for hegemony in spite of the overwhelming military might of the Amerikkkaners? Will an anti-China triple alliance of other upstart East Asian capitalist powers (composed of Japan, South Korea, and Taiwan) successfully join forces with the Amerikkkaners and their NATO allies to prevent China from achieving hegemony (in a manner similar to how the Amerikkkaners joined the British to prevent Germany from achieving hegemony)? If so, will the Amerikkkaners and their NATO allies, having pivoted to Asia, effectively become the imperial military muscle for the resulting capitalist hegemony of the East Asian triple alliance (in a manner similar to how the Spanish and Portuguese effectively provided the imperial military muscle for the capitalist hegemony of the Genoese)?

All very good questions, yes, but Arrighi's book does not invite the reader to ask what I regard to be the most important question today... How can today's anti-imperialists and anti-capitalists force a break with evolutionary patterns of world capitalism that have already inspired and shaped more than five centuries of increasingly devastating genocidal, ethnocidal, and ecocidal projects, and which are presently inspiring and shaping even more devastating genocidal, ethnocidal, and ecocidal projects?

Cedric Robinson's *Black Marxism* covers the same epic five-century time-span as Arrighi's Long Twentieth Century but, instead of focusing on the forces driving the actions of capitalist imperialists, Robinson focuses on the forces driving the actions of the anti-imperialists and anti-capitalists of the Black Radical Tradition. In so doing, Robinson's work invites the reader to ask how today's anti-imperialists and anti-capitalists might force a break with the evolutionary patterns of world capitalism by learning from the successes and failures of the many different anti-imperialist and anti-capitalist traditions to which they are heirs.

The astute reader of Robinson's book will realize three things.

First, the reader will realize that escape, fugitivity, desertion, and marronage are some of the powerful but under-appreciated forms of resistance to imperialism and capitalism, and there are incredible traditions of such resistance that we might learn from. Indeed, given that all direct confrontations with and amongst capitalist imperialists today revolve around the prospects of one party using weapons of mass destruction against their rivals, potentially turning Life on Earth into collateral damage, it seems to me that escape, fugitivity, desertion, and marronage are simultaneously the most powerful and least reckless forms of resistance available to anti-imperialists and anti-capitalists today.

Second, the reader will realize that escape, fugitivity, desertion, and marronage have been the conditions of possibility for the emergence of many other forms of anti-imperialist and anti-capitalist resistance. Escape, fugitivity, desertion, and marronage have, historically, created the time and the space for anti-imperialists and anti-capitalists to conduct experiments in organizing alternative economies and ecologies that were, in Robinson's words, "beyond the comprehension and control of the [capitalist imperialist] master class."

Third, the reader will realize that anti-imperialist and anti-capitalist experiments in organizing alternative economies and ecologies should be about (i) recovering the more or less fragmented remnants of cultures that have been subjected to erasure by the advance of capitalist imperialism, (ii) piecing these remnants together, and (iii) (re-)creating these cultures anew. It is a mistake to think that anti-imperialist and anti-capitalist movements have historically been about putting outmoded cultures behind us and constructing brave new worlds. Rather to the contrary, the forces driving the actions of anti-imperialists and anti-capitalists have, more often than not, been the forces that inspire people(s) to remember cultures that have been lost to and destroyed by the advance of capitalist imperialism. Eurocentric Marxisms often fail to grasp this fact insofar as they refuse to look backward and make amends with the past and, instead, choose to focus on forward looking ideals of the "Communist man" as "man of the future." Indeed, Robinson's book turns on Eurocentric Marxisms' refusals to recognize the Black Radical Tradition's concern with (i) recovering the remnants of African cultures that have been subjected to erasure by Euro-Atlantic capitalist imperialists and (re-)creating these African cultures anew.

Afro-futurism, to the degree that it is a spin-off of the Black Radical Tradition, differs from Eurocentric futurism in that it is about (re)creating the African past anew. Afro-futurist works describe and depict futures in which remnants of past African cultures — remnants of African cultures that have been subjected to erasure by Euro-Atlantic capitalist imperialism — are recovered and pieced together in order to (re-)create them anew. In the process of being recovered, repaired, and (re)created anew, these past African cultures are inevitably transformed in such a way that they are no less futuristic than any product of the Eurocentric futurist imagination.

If Eurocentric futurist works are less lively than Afro-futurist works, it is because Eurocentric futurist works assume that cultures that have been subjected to erasure by Euro-Atlantic capitalist imperialism are cultures that are never to be recovered, meaning that the future must be the product of processes of cultural selection and curation that are governed by modern Euro-Atlantic sensibilities. *How boring!*

Afro-futurist works focus on the (re-)creation of past African cultures anew, yes, but the liveliness of Afro-futurist works arises from the fact that Afro-futurist works effectively assume that ALL of the different cultures subjected to erasure by Euro-Atlantic capitalist imperialism may be recovered and (re-)created anew, not just the pre-modern African cultures but also the pre-modern Asian cultures, the pre-modern Oceanian cultures, the pre-modern New World Indigenous cultures, and the pre-modern matriarchal pagan cultures of Europe.

The Black Radical Tradition is extremely significant because Eurocentric white supremacy and anti-Black racism have been part and parcel of Euro-Atlantic capitalist imperialism since its inception. Indeed, Eurocentric white supremacy and anti-Black racism persist to this day, in spite of the so-called "abolition" of slavery during the late nineteenth century, and they still continue to contribute to the maintenance and advancement of capitalist imperialism. It is true that as the capitalist imperialist struggle for hegemony has pivoted from the Euro-Atlantic to the Asia-Pacific region, the prevalence of Euro-centric white-supremacy has been attenuated to some degree. However, anti-blackness has not been attenuated to nearly the same degree. Indeed, despite the ongoing pivot from the Euro-Atlantic to the Asia-Pacific, race is poised to continue to serve as capitalist imperialism's epistemology, ordering principle, organizing structure, moral authority, and economy of justice, commerce, and power.

Arrighi does not dwell on the racialized Atlantic slave trade in his book, but Arrighi does note (i) that the Genoese financed and the Iberians operated the racialized Atlantic slave trade during their hegemony, (ii) that the Dutch seized control of the racialized Atlantic slave trade from the Iberians when they achieved hegemony, (iii) that the British and the French seized control of the racialized Atlantic slave trade from the Dutch as they competed to assume hegemony, and (iv) that Amerikkkaner wealth was largely built on the exploitation of Black slave laborers acquired through the Atlantic slave trade. This is to say, in other words, that all of the capitalist imperialist hegemons to date have made their fortunes, in part, from the racialized Atlantic slave trade. The racialized Atlantic slave trade may be no more but it effectively set the stage and the template for the exploitative extraction of resources from Africa by anti-Black capitalist imperialists. Ay, all of today's would-be capitalist imperialist hegemons seem more than happy to carry on with the practice of exploiting and extracting resources from Africa, under the auspices of anti-Black logics.

Consider the history of the region known today as the Democratic Republic of Congo, the land that rests upon the craton at the heart of Africa and the land that my maternal ancestors call home.

During the heyday of the Atlantic slave trade, the Long Sixteenth and Seventeenth Centuries, nearly half of the millions disappeared from Africa to the New World as slaves are known to have come from in and around the Congo region, more than from any other region in Africa; millions more died in and around Congo while being marched from the interior to the coast and held in slave prisons, never embarking to the New World; and more millions were never properly enslaved but killed to create the conditions for the slave trade to prosper.

During the Long Nineteenth Century, the concert of European powers that carved up Africa at the Berlin Conference acquiesced to much of the Congo region becoming private property, a giant slave plantation, owned by Belgium's King Leopold, who oversaw a brutal regime of resource extraction and genocide that killed 10 million people, nearly half of the remaining population of the region.

During the Long Twentieth Century, after Congo gained its independence from Belgium, the Amerikkkaners backed a coup d'etat that resulted in three decades of further impoverishment and degradation, with millions more "murdered by omission," while the Amerikkkaner-backed dictatorship of Mobutu Sese Seko oversaw the exploitative extraction of mineral resources from Congo. Subsequently, after Mobutu Sese Seko was deposed, the United Settlers and other capitalist imperialist powers continued to profit from the exploitative extraction of mineral resources from Congo by warlords while more than 6 million more people died in the Congo Wars, the deadliest global conflicts since World War II.

Today, Congo is one of the poorest nations on the planet. More than 30 million people in Congo, approximately a third of the population, are "food insecure," but Congo also happens to be the source of much of the minerals necessary to build the information technologies that are driving capitalist imperialism's growth as it pivots from the Euro-Atlantic to the Asia-Pacific.

At each pivotal juncture of the more than five-hundred years of history that I have briefly related here, proceeding right on up to the present day, capitalist imperialists of all stripes and colors have cited anti-Black logics to either justify or overlook their rapacious behavior towards the people of Congo.

Robinson's focus on the Black Radical Tradition is extremely significant because, given the historical and organic relationships between capitalism, imperialism, anti-Black racism, and the extraction of resources from Africa, it is necessary for every authentically anti-imperialist and anti-capitalist project today to become confluent with the Black Radical Tradition and, vice versa, for the Black Radical Tradition to become confluent with every authentically anti-imperialist and anti-capitalist project. Black lives will matter to anti-imperialist and anti-capitalist projects and, vice versa, the project of making Black lives matter will be an anti-imperialist and anti-capitalist project — that, or neither will be.

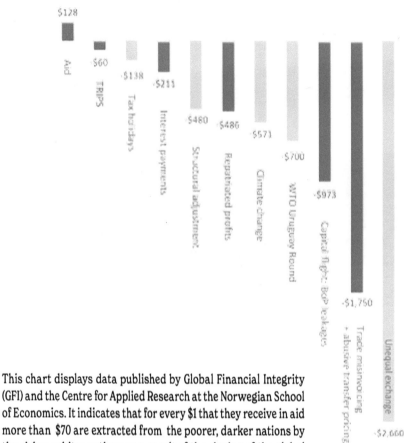

ANNUAL GAINS FROM AID VS. SELECTED
OUTFLOWS & STRUCTURAL COSTS/LOSSES
($US BILLIONS)

$128 — Aid
$60 — TRIPS
-$138 — Tax holidays
-$211 — Interest payments
-$480 — Structural adjustment
-$486 — Repatriated profits
-$571 — Climate change
-$700 — WTO Uruguay Round
-$973 — Capital flight: BoP leakages
-$1,750 — Trade misinvoicing + abusive transfer pricing
-$2,660 — Unequal exchange

This chart displays data published by Global Financial Integrity (GFI) and the Centre for Applied Research at the Norwegian School of Economics. It indicates that for every $1 that they receive in aid more than $70 are extracted from the poorer, darker nations by the richer, whiter nations as a result of the rigging of the global economy.

UNPAYABLE DEBT

& THE ASSASSINATION OF THE THIRD WORLD

In Vijay Prashad's words, "The Third World was not a place. It was a project."
European imperialism and racial capitalism were, as Adom Getachew has observed, "world-constituting forces" that "violently inaugurated an unprecedented era of globality."

Suffering in the wake of the advance of these forces, anti-colonial nationalists from Africa, Asia, Latin America and the Caribbean dreamt of an alternative anti-imperialist global order, and they organized to realize it. To quote Prashad:

> From the rubble of World War II rose a bipolar Cold War that threatened the existence of humanity. Hair-triggers on nuclear weapons alongside heated debates about poverty, inequality, and freedom threatened even those who did not live under the US or Soviet umbrellas. [...] Almost unmolested by the devastation of the war, the United States used its advantages to rebuild the two sides of Eurasia and cage in a battered Soviet Union. Phrases like "massive retaliation" and "brinkmanship" provided no comfort to the two-thirds of the world's people who had only recently won or were on the threshold of winning their independence from colonial rulers.
>
> Thrown between these two major formations, the darker nations amassed as the Third World. Determined people struck out against colonialism to win their freedom. They demanded political equality on the world level. The main institution for this expression was the United Nations. From its inception in 1948, the United Nations played an enormous role for the bulk of the planet. Even if they did not earn permanent seats on the UN Security Council, the new states took advantage of the UN General Assembly to put forward their demands. The Afro-Asian meetings in Bandung and Cairo (1955 and 1961, respectively), the creation of the Non-Aligned Movement in Belgrade (1961), and the Tri-continental Conference in Havana (1966) rehearsed the major arguments within the Third World project so that they could take them in a concerted way to the main stage, the United Nations. In addition, the new states pushed the United Nations to create institutional platforms for their Third World agenda.... Through these institutions, aspects other than political equality came to the fore: the Third World project included a demand for the redistribution of the world's resources, a more dignified rate of return for the labor power of their people, and a shared acknowledgment of the heritage of science, technology, and culture.

The Third World project was an unsuccessful one. Over the course of the Long Twentieth Century, Empire, under Amerikkkan hegemony, responded to the Third World project by sabotaging attempts to create reparative, ant-colonial institutional platforms through the United Nations and by instituting a global apartheid regime that cast nationality as proxy for race. This "assassination" of the Third World anti-colonial project was carried out according to an analytics of raciality that was consistent with Amerikkkan anti-blackness and settler colonialism. A highly stratified internal formation of ethno-racial classes and a ruthless internal hostility towards indigeneity, combined with the massive size of its internal territories, both primed the United Settlers for taking on the role of Imperial hegemon, and shaped their take on this role. This is to say, in other words, that the assassination of the Third World project, and the global apartheid that was its effective result, bear the signatures and hallmarks of the leading conspirator in the design and execution of the assassination.

The global (inter-national) apartheid regime that has emerged under United Settler hegemony effectively deploys nationality as a proxy for race in a manner fitting with the intra-national racial hierarchy found within the United Settler States. Indigenous peoples without nation-states of their own have effectively been excluded from the inter-national racial hierarchy and are deemed expendable to the global economic order. Those nations mostly populated by peoples said to belong to the "Negro" race — i.e., Black Africans and Caribbean Islanders — have been placed at the bottom of the inter-national racial hierarchy, still effectively regarded as socially dead, as slave stock. After the nations of Black Africa and the Caribbean, come the darker nations populated by peoples of the "coolie" races of Asia — a "conglomeration of racial imaginings that emerged worldwide in the era of slave emancipation, a product of the [white] imaginers rather than the [non-whites] imagined". Amerikkkan racists regard the "coolies" of Asia to be a more "dependable" labor force than the "Negroes" of Africa and the Caribbean. After the African and Caribbean "Negroes" and the Asian "coolies", come the settler colonial nations of Latin America whose peoples are demeaned and denigrated by white Amerikkkaners who look down upon Latin America's "alloyed whites," remarking upon their "racial impurities" and "poor racial hygiene," as evinced by prevalent and highly visible populations of "mestizos," "pardos," and "mulattos" amongst them.

In sum, the global (inter-national) apartheid regime that has emerged under United Settler States hegemony puts the White nations of Europe and the Anglophone settler colonies on top; it puts the Black nations of Africa and the Caribbean at the bottom; it excludes Native Americans and other Indigenous peoples without nation-states from consideration and drives them to extinction; it compels the nations of Asian "coolies" to compete amongst themselves and against Latin American nations (deemed to be "polluted" by "mestizos," "pardos," and "mulattos") in order to prove themselves more "dependable" subordinates; and, lastly, it fractions off "talented tenths" from all of the different non-white populations identified above and bestows "honorary whiteness" upon them provided that they offer dependable and loyal service as proxies and redeemers for white-supremacy. Exceptional in this last regard is the nation of Japan and the nations formed from the two crown jewels of Japan's former Asia-Pacific empire, South Korea and Taiwan, which have been granted "honorary white" status as entire nations, in accord with Apartheid South African conventions, because their governments and their business leaders have dependably invested in the maintenance and advancement of United Settler States led Empire and acquiesced to an abject dependence upon the military might of the United Settler States for their survival.

Unpayable debt, as Denise Ferreira da Silva has written, is crucial to the maintenance of this inter-national racial hierarchy. To understand the workings of unpayable debt, just consider the following news headline published in the Guardian on the 3rd of February 2023, "Ontario says 'colonization' costs mean it does not owe First Nations billions." Effectively, the government of Ontario in Canada has argued in court that, "It was costly for us to displace and genocide Native peoples and to wreck their lands to satisfy our needs. The costs of our deathly colonial enterprise cannot be borne by us as colonizers alone. The colonized whom we displaced and genocided are responsible for a large part of these costs." Many white Amerikkkaners believe the same about slavery and respond likewise to demands for reparations, "Enslaving Africans for four centuries then instituting a *de jure* apartheid regime against them for another century following emancipation was costly for white Amerikkkaners: enslaved Africans and their descendants are responsible for a large part of these costs." Writ large, one finds that this cruel miscomprehension is crucial to the maintenance of a global (inter-national) racial hierarchy following the same logic, "Euro-Atlantic racism, colonialism, and imperialism was a costly endeavor for the white-supremacists, colonizers, and imperialists of the Euro-Atlantic, and the victims of racism, colonialism, and imperialism are largely responsible for the costliness of these endeavors."

Going further and digging deeper, it is worth quoting Silva on the circumstances that brought the figure of unpayable debt to her attention:

This image first came to me as I was trying to make sense of how those who lacked equity [and] had been forced to take on loans with exorbitant (variable) interest were blamed for the global economic crisis of 2007-8. Holders of subprime loans, Black and Latinx economically dispossessed persons, were presented in explanations for the crisis as profitable (economically) because their anticipated inability to pay made the loans more valuable. However, when that inability was realized, and the abstract financial instruments of which they were part vaporized, these Black and Latinx persons were found responsible (ethically) for the near collapse of the global economy.

In an all too similar manner, lacking equity in the global economic order, the darker nations have been forced to take on loans with exorbitant interest rates. Loans to the darker nations are considered profitable because they will never be fully paid off and creditors can reap the fees and interest on these loans in perpetuity. That being said, however, the loans remain profitable only provided that the darker nations can make the minimum payments needed to service the loans in perpetuity. When the darker nations fail to make their minimum payments, they threaten to undermine the basis of the global economy. This is to say, in other words, that the darker nations are being held ethically responsible for maintaining a global neocolonial economic system that denigrates and exploits them.

In the aftermath of the Civil War, the United Settler States deployed this very same logic of unpayable debt against the newly emancipated slaves, setting the template for many future deployments. It is worth quoting Saidiya Hartman writing in *Scenes of Subjection* on this exemplary deployment of unpayable debt:

Emancipation instituted indebtedness. Blame and duty and blood and dollars marked the birth of the free(d) subject. The very bestowal of freedom established the indebtedness of the freed through a calculus of blame and responsibility that mandated that the formerly enslaved both repay this investment of faith and prove their worthiness. The temporal attributes of indebtedness bind one to the past, since what is owed draws the past into the present, and suspends the subject between what has been and what is. In this regard, indebtedness confers durability, for the individual is answerable to and liable for past actions and must be abstinent in the present in the hopes of securing the future. [...] Debt was at the center of a moral economy of submission and servitude and was instrumental in the production of peonage. Above all, it operated to bind the subject by compounding the service owed, augmenting the deficit through interest accrued, and advancing credit that extended interminably the obligation of service. The emancipated were introduced to the circuits of exchange through the figurative deployment of debt, which obliged them to both enter coercive contractual relations and faithfully remunerate the treasure expended on their behalf. Furthermore, debt literally sanctioned bondage and propelled the freed toward indentured servitude by the selling off of future labor. [...] Thus the transition from slavery to freedom introduced the free agent to the circuits of exchange through this construction of already accrued debt, an abstinent present, and a mortgaged future. In short, to be free was to be a debtor — that is, obliged and duty-bound to others.

The circumstances of the slave turned freeman upon emancipation is iso-morphic to the situation of the colony turned free nation upon decolonization. The transition from colony to free nation introduced the postcolonial nation to the circuits of exchange, likewise through the construction of already accrued debt, an abstinent present, and a mortgaged future. In short, to be a free postco-lonial nation is to be a debtor nation — that is, (ethically) obliged and duty-bound to uphold a neocolonial world order that cruelly exploits postcolonial nations for (economic) profit.

It is important to recognize, however, that it is not being indebted that burdens the darker nations in our post-colonial/neo-colonial era but, more pro-foundly, it is the fact that the terms of their indebtedness bind the darker nations to a global order that exploits them. The whiter nations of Empire's core are also debtor nations, but their debts bind them to a global order that privileges them. The richer, whiter nations of the imperialist white-supremacist capitalist patri-archal core, led by the United Settlers, effected their assassination of the Third World project by saddling the darker nations of the periphery with unpayable debts whose terms (ethically) bound them to the maintenance and advancement of a global (economic) order that privileged the richer, whiter nations of the core and stratified the poorer, darker nations of the periphery according to an analytics of raciality that was distinctively anti-black. The darker nations were compelled to take on such unpayable debts under extreme duress, upon being visited by one or more of the Four Horsemen of Empire: disease, famine, civil war, and foreign intervention. It is by and through unpayable debts that the richer, whiter nations of the core have managed to cruelly exact payments from the darker nations as their due contribution to their own colonization.

The radical Pan-Africanists of the Third World were keenly prescient in pre-dicting this outcome during the Long Twentieth Century. This is because they were deeply familiar with and sensitive to the fact that Empire's new hegemon, the United Settlers, had ruthlessly wielded unpayable debts against peoples of African descent upon their emancipation. The radical Pan-Africanists knew that, the moment the colonized won their independence, the United Settlers would be primed to wield unpayable debts against them according to an analytics of raciality that would force the peoples of Black Africa and the Caribbean to the bottom of the heap.

To interpolate Hartman: [T]*he radical Pan-Africanists predicted that the new postcolonial states would be burdened by fictions of debt premised upon selective and benign representations of colonization that emphasized paternalism, dependency, and will-lessness. Given this rendition of colonization, responsibility would be deemed the best antidote for the ravages of the past; never mind that it effaced the enormity of the injuries of the past, entailed the erasure of history, and placed the onus of the past onto the shoulders of individual post-colonial nation-states. Recrimination and punishment were to be the rewards of decolonization. Decolonization would confer sovereignty and autonomy only to abandon the postcolonial nation-state in a self-blaming and penalizing neoliberal world order. In the wake of the assassination of the Third World project, each postcolonial nation-state would become an island unto itself, accountable for its own making and answerable to its failures; geo-political-economic relations would thereby recede before the "will of the nation" and the blameworthy and politically isolated government of the nation-state.*

Ay, and in this way, Black Africa and the Caribbean would effectively remain the lands of the socially dead by another name; their peoples being instructed to pull themselves up by their bootstraps and make do without reparations for centuries of dispossessions and denigrations, for mass kidnappings and the forced deportations of tens of millions, for slavery and social death, for mass slaughters and the organized abandonment of a hundred million and more to disease and famine — directed to forsake any thought of amends for the devastations that shredded the fabric of social life amongst them.

Ontario says 'colonization' costs mean it does not owe First Nations billions

Canadian province argues in court it is not responsible for compensating Indigenous people over broken treaty obligations

📷 A judge ruled five years ago that the Crown broke its pledge, made in two 1850 treaties, to Indigenous peoples Photograph: Kyaw Soe Oo/Reuters

Ontario has claimed that it does not need to pay billions of dollars owed to First Nations over broken treaty obligations, arguing that it has already spent the sum on the historical costs of resource extraction and the infrastructure of "colonization".

Canada's federal government and the province have spent the last week in a Sudbury court arguing neither is responsible for compensating Indigenous nations for more than 150 years of lost revenues.

Five years ago, superior court justice Patricia Hennessey ruled that the Crown broke its pledge, made in two 1850 treaties, that it would increase payments to Indigenous peoples as more natural resources were extracted from their lands.

FOR THE
ANCESTORS

"The tradition of all dead generations weighs like a nightmare on the brains of the living."
— Karl Marx from *The Eighteenth Brumaire of Louis Bonaparte*

"[Because] even the dead will not be safe from the enemy if he wins."
— Walter Benjamin from "On the Concept of History"

"[But] to see the dead as the individuals they once were tends to obscure their nature. Try to consider the living as we might assume the dead to do: collectively. The collective would accrue not only across space but also throughout time. It would include all those who have ever lived. And so we would also be thinking of the dead. The living reduce the dead to those who have lived; yet the dead already include the living in their own great collective.
"[…] How do the living live with the dead? Until the dehumanization of society by capitalism, all the living awaited the experience of the dead. It was their ultimate future. By themselves the living were incomplete. Thus living and dead were interdependent. Always. Only a uniquely modern form of egoism has broken this interdependence. With disastrous results for the living, who now think of the dead as the eliminated."
— John Berger from "Twelve Theses on the Economy of the Dead"

Western(ized) scientists who present themselves to the public as experts in the field of psychology are claiming to have rather recently "discovered" a fact that every "primitive" non-Western person will have been well aware of since early childhood: the fact that the spirits of our ancestors remain with us.

In order to make the claim that they have "discovered" something, these Western(ized) scientists refuse to use "primitivisms" that are sensible and poetic. Instead, they prefer to use banal mannerisms: they speak of "multigenerational family systems" and "stress being transmitted transgenerationally.". These banal mannerisms only serve to help Western(ized) scientists cling to that "uniquely modern form of egoism" that "[reduces] the dead [to] the eliminated".

Why are Western(ized) scientists so desperate to maintain that the dead are those who have been eliminated?

Well, think of it this way, if the dead victims of Western civilization's genocidal conquests are still with us, then the West could be said to owe these dead victims apologies and reparations. But if these victims have been eliminated and are no longer with us, then it is meaningless to apologize and make reparations to them.

What's more, if the dead perpetrators of all the genocides, ethnocides, and ecocides that constitute Western civilization's conquests are still with us, then these dead perpetrators ought to be confronted and challenged to apologize and make reparations to their victims in the name of truth and reconciliation. But if these perpetrators have been eliminated and are no longer with us, then it is meaningless to confront and challenge them.

When communing with the dead — no matter whether it is to confront and challenge, or make amends, or express gratitude — the most common mistake is, as John Berger writes, "to see the dead as the individuals they once were," for this "tends to obscure their nature." Whenever the Western(ized) scientist scoffs at the "primitive" non-Westerner who defers to the spirits of their ancestors, you will find that the Western(ized) scientist is purposefully making this very mistake: they are presuming that the "primitive" non-Westerner is saying that each and every one of their individual ancestors exists in the present as a spirit that is in touch with them directly. When talking about "stress transmitted transgenerationally," it is often more sensible and more poetic for one to say "I can sense my anxious mother's spirit in the room" even though one knows very well that, thinking literally, one is talking about a situation triggering stress that has been communicated transgenerationally to one's own person via one's late mother. Western(ized) scientists take such figurative sayings literally in order to make "primitive" non-Westerners out to be superstitious fools, but Western(ized) scientists are, in fact, fooling themselves in order to avoid the truth of what is being said so poetically and sensibly by the "primitive" non-Westerner. To add insult to injury, when compelled to admit the truth of such a "primitivism," the Western(ized) scientist will proceed to make an elaborate show of explicating all that was obviously implicit in the "primitivism" in order to claim to have made a "scientific discovery" or a "theoretical breakthrough."

It is as if I said to you, "Your wool coat is in the closet." And then you were to respond to me, "You silly fool. My wool coat is not simply in the closet; it is, scientifically speaking, hanging on a coat hanger in the closet along with five other coats that are not my wool coat." You would hardly be surprised if I clucked my tongue at you and told you to fuck off.

We who are not afraid of being called "(neo)primitives," – we who sensibly and poetically speak of "our ancestors remaining with us" — read the "latest" psychological findings on "multi-generational family systems," cluck our tongues at the overwrought verbiage and the scrupulous efforts to avoid "primitivisms" that make sense and poetry, and we say, "Get the fuck outta here!" We do the same when we read climate science reports that avoid sensible and poetic "primitivisms" like "care for the forest that feeds you" in favor of banal mannerisms like "engage in sustainable agroforestry."

Too many "civilized" and "modern" people speak dismissively of "primitive ancestor cults" and imagine that all "primitive" peoples worship and serve their ancestors like "civilized" peoples do monarchs, oligarchs, Big Gods, and other imperialist patriarchs. Too few regard "primitive" practices closely enough and think about them deeply enough to recognize their psychological sophistication. Those who thoughtlessly dismiss "primitive superstitions" regarding ancestral spirits are refusing to comprehend matters: these so-called "superstitious practices" are, more often than not, sophisticated devices for recognizing and healing what psychologists have recently come to recognize as chronic stresses and traumas transmitted transgenerationally.

If Western(ized) scientists are now making a show of explicating some of what was obviously implicit in non-Western(ized) others' observations regarding ancestral spirits, it is because there is now something to be profitably extracted from those observations. Indeed, what has happened is this: the transgenerational transmission of chronic stresses and traumas has become so acute in our time that there is a growing market for treating those who are suffering from these chronic stresses and traumas. The aim of Western(ized) psychology is not at all to heal chronic stresses and traumas that have been transmitted through the generations: the Western(ized) scientist does not want to enable peoples to confront and challenge their cruel ancestors nor seek reparations for their suffering ancestors. Rather, the aim of Western(ized) psychology is to find better ways to "manage" the transgenerational transmission of chronic stresses and traumas without ever enabling peoples to heal them. palliative treatment instead of curative treatment.

Increased exposure to chronic stresses and psychological traumas sickens and eventually kills us. This is a recent "discovery" claimed by scientists in the burgeoning field psycho-immuno-neuro-endocrinology. But imperialist patriarchies have known this to be true for millennia. Ay, for some five hundred years, imperialist white-supremacist capitalist patriarchy has, far more than any other imperialist patriarchy, excelled at using chronic stresses and psychological traumas to sicken and to kill those it oppresses. To use sensible and poetic terms, imperialist white-supremacist capitalist patriarchy has especially excelled at preventing the living from communing with the dead, so that chronic stresses and psychological traumas are communicated transgenerationally without ever healing.

All imperialisms work by filtering and channeling differing social elements apart from one another, making it increasingly burdensome and unappealing for differing social elements to commune fluently with one another, and making it more practical and appealing for some social elements to dominate, exploit, and eliminate others. Borrowing a term coined by Achille Mbembe, "necropolitical" imperialisms are those that filter and channel the living apart from the dead (including those cast as "socially dead"), and make it practical and appealing for the living to regard the dead as the eliminated. There is no curative psychotherapy for today's prevailing stresses and traumas that does not involve countering today's ruling necropolitical imperialisms; a psychotherapy that does not aim to counter necropolitical imperialisms can only ever provide palliative care. Countering necropolitical imperialisms means making it increasingly easy and appealing for the living and the dead to confluence and commune with one another: not so that the living and the dead differ any less from one another but, rather to the contrary, so that the living and the dead come to defer more to one another despite differing. To recognize this is to recognize that what many Western(ized) anthropologists have called practices in and through which the living "venerate" the dead are better understood as practices for (re-)creating "mutual deferences" amongst the living and the dead, involving confrontations, challenges, and reparations in addition to or as opposed to venerations.

Early 20th century Nkisi N'Kondi figure
by Kongo artist and nganga (ritual practitioner)

RUNNING THOUGHTS ON TRAUMA

I.

Global apartheid and planetary ecocide are here, now. The reckless disregard for life that has brought us to this point has been called inexplicable by some and inevitable by others, but I find that it is neither inexplicable nor inevitable. As I see it, all of the various rationales being deployed to explain and to justify people's inability to care about so many ongoing genocides, ethnocides, and ecocides are themselves, in fact, the symptoms of anxieties that stem from various sorts of traumas.

In a book titled *Inhibitions, Symptoms, and Anxiety*, Freud proposed that our egos produce anxiety in us in order to keep us from spontaneously acting in ways that our egos anticipate will cause us harm. Our egos do this by calling to mind images of past experiences that (dis)simulate anticipated harms before they actually take place. Sometimes the images that our egos call to mind evoke traumatic events from our past. When traumas are evoked, our super-egos enter the mix and censor the images recalled, repressing and distorting these images before they fully come to mind. The effective result is this: on the one hand, our egos recall images that provoke feelings of anxiety in us and keep us from acting spontaneously; on the other hand, our super-egos repress and distort what is recalled so that we cannot properly make sense of what we are anxious about. Unable to make sense of what we are anxious about, we proceed to rationalize our inability to act spontaneously—that is to say, in other words, that we come up with abstract reasons to explain why we shouldn't act spontaneously.

The person who has been traumatized is often, but not always, a person who is unable to spontaneously act in caring ways because they have come to anticipate that caring will cause them harm. Whenever the traumatized person feels the urge to care for themselves or to care for others, their egos call to mind images of experiences that have taught them to associate caring for themselves or others with harm but, at the same time, their super-egos repress and distort the images called to mind. The effective result is this: the traumatized person is apprehensive about spontaneously caring, but they cannot make sense of what has made them apprehensive about caring. In lieu of making sense of their inability to spontaneously care, the traumatized person will come up with abstract reasons to explain why they shouldn't spontaneously care.

Anyone and everyone who uses abstract reasoning to justify denying themselves or others care is a traumatized person engaged in rationalizing their apprehensions. Freudian psychoanalysis teaches us that the only sensible justifications for denying care to oneself or to another are to be found in one's concrete experiences, and not in one's abstract reasoning. Thus, it is imperative (i) that we dismiss the abstract reasoning that we use to justify our inability to care and (ii) that we uncover the concrete experiences that we are simultaneously recollecting and repressing whenever we have inhibitions about caring.

My point here is this: the way to get peoples to affirm ideological or mythical reasons for denying care to themselves and others is to (i) traumatize peoples in some way shape or form, (ii) allow their traumas to fester unresolved for an extended duration, and then (iii) play upon their traumas. All genocidal, ethnocidal, and ecocidal power formations work by exposing differing social elements to different types of traumas in order to prevent these differing elements from properly caring for one another and from mixing and mingling together — this is what makes it possible for one social element to endeavor to dominate and eliminate others for ideological or mythical reasons.

Imperialist white-supremacist capitalist patriarchy, the power formation driving global apartheid and planetary ecocide, works to stratify societies by race, by sex, and by economic class, and it does so by exposing individuals of differing races, sexes, and economic classes to different traumas — all so that (i) these differing sorts of individuals are no longer able to properly defer to and care for one another and (ii) these differing sorts of individuals will affirm racist, sexist, and classist ideologies and myths that rationalize their inability to properly care for one another. Speak to anyone who is indifferent to, or actively engaged in, the maintenance and advancement of global apartheid and planetary ecocide, and you will sooner or later find them ascribing to racist, sexist, and classist ideologies and myths. Proceed to put them on the couch and under analysis and you will, time and time again, discover that the ideologies and myths they ascribe to are symptoms of their traumas.

II.

The Freudian two-step for treating traumas runs as follows: (i) get the traumatized individual to recognize that their rationalizations for not caring for themselves and others are covering up traumas, then (ii) get the traumatized individual to become aware of the traumas that they are simultaneously recollecting and repressing whenever they have inhibitions about caring for themselves and others. This Freudian two-step is a good start, but it doesn't go far enough.

Following in the footsteps of Frantz Fanon, Gilles Deleuze, Felix Guattari and others, we need take matters one step further: we need the traumatized individual to recognize whether it is and how it is that their trauma was produced by a process of traumatization that serves a prevailing power formation. That is to say that the traumatized individual has to discover whether or not they have been traumatized in order to maintain social stratification, in order to ensure that individuals belonging to differing social groups refrain from mixing and mingling together, and do not spontaneously care for one another. The third step in the treatment of trauma that I am advocating points to the fact that, unless the power formations that stratify societies are countered and their attendant processes of traumatization are terminated, the individual who resolves a given trauma will, sooner or later, be re-traumatized as a result of the workings of power formations that stratify societies.

Let us take, for example, the proliferation of white male mass shooters in the United Settler States, which points to the specific manner in which certain kinds of white males are exposed to certain kinds of traumas that prevent them from caring for the lives of others. If we mean to solve this problem, we cannot trust those who do nothing more than critique the ideologies and myths that white male mass shooters ascribe to. Nor can we trust those who ask us to do nothing more than empathize with individual white male mass shooters and to consider their traumas. Those we can trust are those who go deep, and situate the traumas endured by white male mass shooters within the context of a society dominated by white-supremacist capitalist patriarchal power formations. What we need to do above all else is expose the fact that the white male mass shooter's traumas are the product of white supremacist and patriarchal power formations that aim to encourage him to dominate and eliminate others instead of care for others. Ay, we need to expose the fact that others, Black and indigenous peoples in particular, are being traumatized concomitantly, by related power formations, in order to keep them from caring for themselves and to make them accept being dominated and eliminated by white men. What's more, we need to recognize that there is no dealing with the traumas of the oppressor without dealing with the traumas of the oppressed: there is no treating the traumas of the potential white male mass shooter without also treating the traumas of those whom he is most likely to target, for these traumas are conditioned by deeply interlocked concatenations of power formations.

III.

My thinking on the matter of trauma assumes that caring for ourselves and others is our default setting. That being said, I find that none of us can care equally for everything everywhere all at once. At any given moment in time, each of us has to prioritize caring for some peoples, places, and things over and above others. But it is important not to confuse prioritizing this person, place, or thing over that person, place, or thing with claiming that this person, place, or thing deserves care while that person, place, or thing deserves indifference or abuse. "Over and above" is not synonymous with "over and against."

Self-care is about attending to the ever evolving limits of one's ability to care for others and learning how to prioritize who or what to care for within one's limits at any given moment in time, so as to avoid burning out. The choice of what to prioritize is rarely a rational choice, but a matter of being more or less affectively enchanted by peoples, places, and things, and lured to care for them. The abstract reasons that you cite in order to explain and justify your priorities are only ever symptoms of the degree to which you find some people, places, and things more enchanting and alluring than others.

Processes of traumatization work to shape our affects so as to make us become utterly enchanted or utterly disenchanted by certain kinds of persons, places, things — the effective result being that certain persons, places, things acquire an extreme allure while others lose their allure almost entirely. To say that X doesn't deserve any care but, instead, deserves indifference or abuse is to have been traumatized against caring for X. Concomitantly, to say in that X "is the only thing in the world worth caring for" is to have been traumatized in such a way that one cares for "X" to an extreme degree — the term for this sort of extreme caring-for being a "trauma bond." Those who care for certain people, places, or things to such an extreme degree that they succumb to burnout are likely to have been trauma-bonded to that for which they show extreme care and, at the same time, traumatized so as to become indifferent or abusive to themselves.

People who have overcome traumas are much more sensible about caring. They will say, "Given that I can only care so much at any given time, and given that X is presently the most enchanting and alluring person, place, or thing to me now, I am presently prioritizing X. But this doesn't mean that X is the only thing that I care for right now. I presently care more for X and less for everything else besides, yes, but I still do care for everything else besides to varying lesser degrees.

Some things will matter more to me at any given time, but everything matters to me. Priority is not a synonym for exclusivity."

What's more, people who have overcome traumas are open and honest about their priorities being determined by their sensibilities. When asked why they have prioritized this person, place, or thing over others, people who have overcome traumas will remark upon their sensibilities and the formative experiences that have shaped their sensibilities, including traumatic experiences. They will neither claim to be making rational calculations nor claim to be upholding moral principles. Going further, people who have overcome traumas will situate their many formative experiences in their differing social contexts, attending to the power formations prevailing over differing social contexts. "Let me share with you the experiences that have led me to prioritize X and put these experiences in context for you."

IV.

To use my self as an example, my personal apprehensions and anxieties around meritocratic distinctions can be traced back to the trauma of being routinely beaten as a child for having failed to behave and achieve in a manner that would mark me as a Black person of distinction, not just another Black person in Amerikkka. To situate my trauma in its proper social context, I must attend to the power formations that work to traumatize Black children so that they will grow into adults who have difficulty caring for themselves, who feel that their failure to live up to "superior" standards of "achievement" set by rich white men is a mark against them that justifies their being subject to injury and death as unintended consequence of routine disciplinary action, as normalized accident, and as collateral damage of society's pursuit of progressive optimization.

Going further and digging deeper, however, I must recognize my trauma is not simply my own: it is an ancestral trauma. Colonialism brought new deprivations and new logics of corporal punishment to Africa, and my father, his father, and his father's father were all traumatized into accepting the fact that any Black person lacking in distinction, who did not submit to administration and supervision by the colonizer, was liable to be killed by the workings of the colonial administration, sometimes by its malice (i.e., murder by commission) but more often by its neglect (i.e., murder by omission). My father was an acute victim of this ancestral trauma for having been born during the post-WWII famines and shortages in Tanzania, and he transmitted his own ancestral traumas to me by beating them into my flesh. I know from others, however, that his physical abuse was not really necessary to transmit such a trauma to me: emotional abuse and emotional unavailability can transmit ancestral traumas from generation to generation even more effectively, thanks to their greater subtleties.

This is the rub. Imperialist white-supremacist capitalist patriarchy, having been around for more than five centuries now, no longer needs to directly inflict fresh traumas upon the flesh of its victims in order to oppress and dominate its victims. Instead, imperialist white-supremacist capitalist patriarchy can indirectly traumatize its victims by facilitating the transmission of ancestral traumas from generation to generation in subtle waves. Of course, imperialist white-supremacist capitalist patriarchy has never ceased to inflict fresh traumas upon its victims, but it has, for a long time, relied heavily upon the perpetuation of ancestral traumas in order to perpetuate itself. As I have already noted, one of the primary means by which imperialist white-supremacist capitalist patriarchy sickens and kills people today is by facilitating the transmission of chronic stresses and psychological traumas transgenerationally while, at the same time, making it increasingly difficult for peoples to heal transgenerational stresses and traumas by communing with their dead ancestors.

Returning to the problem of the white male mass shooter, the traumas that encourage him to dominate and exterminate others are, no doubt, ancestral traumas that have encouraged generations of men before him to actively participate in or passively acquiesce to white-supremacist capitalist patriarchal projects of genocide, ethnocide, and ecocide. There is no solving the problem of the white male mass shooter without healing his ancestral traumas, his "White Man's Burden." Gun control measures may lessen the symptoms of his ancestral traumas, but gun control measures will never heal them. When guns are unavailable, traumatized white males will seek alternative means to commit acts of extreme violence as long as their ancestral traumas render them incapable of caring for others, and as long as their potential victims are suffering from ancestral traumas that encourage them to accept being dominated and exploited.

Indeed, with this in mind, we need to recognize that a sizable number of white men are only waiting for a "legitimate" reason to perpetrate or participate in mass murder. The white male mass shooter is but one who ceases to wait to be given a "legitimate" reason by authorities, and acts to legitimate his own reason. Most white men with an inclination to mass murder can, and are, waiting for authorities to provide them with a reason to act, satisfying their murderous urges in the interim playing shoot'em up games, watching shoot 'em up films, and firing guns at shooting ranges. No matter whether they are waiting to be given reasons or making their own reasons, a sizable number of white Amerikkkaner men are suffering from a trans-generation repetition compulsion that is driving them to reenact the cruelties of their genocidal ancestors. Ay, and we need to recognize that most white Amerikkkaner men who are inclined towards mass murder by their ancestral traumas are not engaging in acts of mass murder by commission, like mass shootings, but, instead, are engaging in acts of mass murder by omission, by either actively participating in or passively acquiescing to projects of organized abandonment that result in mass deaths.

We need to recognize that enacting the third step in the treatment of trauma — recognizing the extent to which one's trauma has been produced by a process of traumatization that serves a prevailing power formation — must involve recognizing the extent to which what appears to be one's own trauma is, in fact, an ancestral trauma that has been transmitted down through the generations.

V.

Most of the examples cited in these running thoughts on trauma could be said to deal with human beings who have been traumatized into denying care to other human beings and denying care to themselves as human beings. What concerns me most, however, are the ways in which human beings are traumatized into denying care to non-human others and denying care to what they view to be the non-human parts of themselves. I believe that there is no way to counter the planetary ecocide that defines our time without recognizing that this ecocide is being perpetrated and perpetuated by human beings who refuse to care for non-human others, and who treat non-human others with indifference or abuse.

Of course, the traumas that prevent humans from caring for one another cannot be disentangled from those that prevent humans from caring for non-humans. This becomes obvious to anyone who considers the fact that humans who have been traumatized against caring for other humans often rationalize their inhibitions by claiming that other humans are "less human" than they are. Indeed, it is a legal principle in much of the Western(ized) world that the less human you are, the less care you deserve — rights and privileges are given to non-human others when they are sufficiently "humanized" and, vice versa, rights and privileges are denied to humans when they are sufficiently "dehumanized." But this legal principle is but a symptom of so many traumatic experiences that have warped Western(ized) people's sensibilities in such a way that they have become indifferent and abusive towards dehumanized and non-human others.

I often ask myself the following question. "Why must Western(ized) anthropologists speak of 'primitive' peoples living in 'small foraging bands' when the peoples they are referring to can and do live as if they are part of immense and complex societies that involve great multitudes of sentient non-human others?"

These running thoughts on trauma have led me to an answer to this question. As I see it now, Western(ized) anthropologists refuse to respect "primitive" peoples' claims to live in societies that include multitudes of non-human others because these anthropologists are rationalizing traumas that have made them apprehensive about caring for dehumanized and non-human others.

But what are the processes of traumatization that have traumatized Western(ized) peoples against caring for dehumanized and non-human others? To what degree are these processes of traumatization currently inflicting fresh traumas upon their victims and to what degree are they facilitating the transmission of ancestral traumas from generation to generation? And how precisely do these processes of traumatization contribute to power formations that maintain and advance social stratification within the Western(ized) world, within that deathly world of suffering over which imperialist white-supremacist capitalist patriarchy prevails?

White Amerikkkaners posing with a mountain of bison skulls. Photo taken in Rougeville, Michigan, in 1892. Amerikkkaner military commanders ordered their troops to kill buffalo to deny Natives an important source of food.

BURNING OUT

"Disciplinary society is a society of negativity. It is defined by the negativity of prohibition. The negative modal verb that governs it is May Not. By the same token, the negativity of compulsion adheres to Should. Achievement society, more and more, is in the process of discarding negativity. Increasing deregulation is abolishing it. Unlimited Can is the positive modal verb of achievement society. Its plural form—the affirmation, "Yes, we can"—epitomizes achievement society's positive orientation. Prohibitions, commandments, and the law are replaced by projects, initiatives, and motivation. Disciplinary society is still governed by no. Its negativity produces madmen and criminals. In contrast, achievement society creates depressives and losers.

" [...] Beyond a certain point of productivity, disciplinary technology—or, alternately, the negative scheme of prohibition—hits a limit. To heighten productivity, the paradigm of disciplination is replaced by the paradigm of achievement, or, in other words, by the positive scheme of Can; after a certain level of productivity obtains, the negativity of prohibition impedes further expansion. The positivity of Can is much more efficient than the negativity of Should. Therefore, the social unconscious switches from Should to Can. The achievement-subject is faster and more productive than the obedience-subject. However, the Can does not revoke the Should. The obedience-subject remains disciplined. It has now completed the disciplinary stage.

" [...] Excess work and performance escalate into auto-exploitation. This is more efficient than allo-exploitation, for the feeling of freedom attends it. The exploiter is simultaneously the exploited. Perpetrator and victim can no longer be distinguished. Such self-referentiality produces a paradoxical freedom that abruptly switches over into violence because of the compulsive structures dwelling within it. The psychic indispositions of achievement society are pathological manifestations of such a paradoxical freedom."
— Byung-Chul Han from *Burnout Society*

I need to admit something — to myself most of all, but to my readers as well — and it is this: I am burning out.

It is important that I admit this to myself and to my readers because, if I am to live by what I write, it is imperative that I do not divorce what I produce from the process of its production.

Over the past five years, I've written, edited, designed, and self-published six books, and I've written many other precis, essays, and occasional pieces besides; I've participated in and conducted seminars that have involved reading tens of thousands of dense pages of philosophy, psychology, and history; I've presented original research and creative projects at panels and workshops at several academic conferences; and I've maintained intellectual dialogues and correspondences with a number of artists, philosophers, and scientists.

Undoubtedly, this work has given my life meaning, so to speak, but it has neither clothed, nor fed, nor sheltered me and my loved ones. To the contrary, this work has, more often than not, drawn upon the scarce economic resources available to me and, in so doing, it has often made it more difficult for me to support myself and my loved ones.

Given that I make experimental and countercultural work on the margins of the academy and the culture industry, rather than being paid, I find that I usually have to pay for access and opportunities to share my work with audiences and with other creatives doing work that complements my own. What's more, I am a first generation African in Amerikkka who is very vulnerable to the depredations of the nation's racist neoliberal economic regime: I have neither family wealth nor legacy connections to networks of cultural and social capital that might enable me to thrive on the countercultural margins. This is to say, in other words, that I must often pay a premium, in both unpaid labor time and money, for access and opportunities that I could already hardly afford.

To make a living for myself and to pay to do the work that gives my life meaning, I have had to hold down several full-time administrative jobs, stealing back what time I can from my employers in order to make time for more meaningful work.

Stealing the time needed to do what I have done over the past five years has been no easy feat for me. It has required time management balancing acts that required that I develop and deploy subtle diplomatic skills in order to delay the biddings, commands, directives, and orders of my "superiors" without rubbing them the wrong way and being (mis)taken for a less than capable and dutiful employee. Stealing time has, thus, been a source of immense stress, compounding the stresses of actually doing the meaningful work that I endeavor to do in my stolen time.

As you know, dear reader, the work that gives my life meaning is the work of uncovering and considering the deeply disturbing realities of prevailing imperialisms in order to conceive of ways to make artful reparations to those who suffer them. This work demands that I deeply consider the murder, rape, starvation, and torture of hundreds of millions of dehumanized humans, and the outrageous cruelties inflicted upon countless non-human others over the past five centuries of advancing imperialist white-supremacist capitalist patriarchal hegemony. These horrors have shaped and continue to shape my own personal history and are part and parcel of an ongoing planetary ecocide, the Great Thinning and the Sixth Extinction.

The fact of the matter is, however, that I am one of the lucky ones. I have been furnished with motives, means, and opportunities to steal time back for myself and to deeply consider my own life circumstances in relation to the ongoing planetary ecocide. Perhaps I can take pride in having seized upon the motives, means, and opportunities that have been made available to me, but I am incredibly lucky that these have been made available to me at all. Such motives, means, and opportunities are not commonly made available, and many today find that the most tolerable life for them is a life in which they dissociate as best they can from the profound genocidal, ethnocidal and ecocidal projects that are ruining life on our planet.

This is all "by design" so to speak. I have been given more motives, means, and opportunities than some because I have been deemed a more tolerable risk for the status quo than some; and I have been given less than others because I have been deemed a less tolerable risk than others. I have proved myself a more tolerable risk to the status quo by ensuring that my work, though not properly academic, is academically inflected, and by making countercultural appeals that are far more intellectual than emotional. I have muted my anger and disgust towards the status quo in order to maintain that I am a "reasonable" critic of the status quo — a critic who does not let his own personal circumstances and his emotional responses get in the way of his rational analyses. The fact of the matter is, however, that I am often overwhelmed by the hysterical anger and obsessive neurotic disgust that I feel towards the status quo, while believing that anger and disgust are a healthy responses to an unhealthy reality. Still, however, I continue to put a great deal of effort into muting my anger and disgust so that I am not dismissed as a maladjusted misfit by gatekeepers who might bar my access to the margins of the academy and culture industry. This is neither a thing to be proud of nor is it a healthy thing to do.

To repress healthy anger and disgust that demands to be expressed and, in so doing, benefit from comforting gatekeepers, is a backhanded form of privilege, yes, but it is a form of privilege nonetheless. The anger and disgust that the status quo evokes in most of us is, justifiably, far too much for many of us to hold back — a fact which has effectively enabled privileged gatekeepers to deny access and opportunities to many "uncivil" Black, colored, and indigenous persons, citing their "behavioral issues." Those among us who are able to hold back and do not ruffle the feathers of gatekeepers need to recognize that this ability is a remarkable privilege.

Before I move on, I need you to feel some of the anger and disgust that I am talking about here. You really must remember this: hundreds of millions of mostly Black, colored, and indigenous people have been murdered, raped, starved, and tortured over the past five centuries in order to construct a world in which wildlife populations, which have already fallen by two-thirds over the last fifty years, continue to fall to new lows; a world in which nearly half of all Earth's languages are endangered and threatened with extinction within a century; a world in which two billion mostly Black, colored, and indigenous people are going hungry and four billion are enduring the grinding poverty of underdevelopment. All that this deathly world of suffering condescends to offer individuals enduring the grinding poverty of underdevelopment (which pulverizes the body) is the slim chance that they or, what is more likely, their descendants might someday graduate to a level of development that will subject them to the draining "modernized poverty" of development (which does not pulverize the body but, instead, saps the spirit and leaves the body feeling empty and meaningless). As Ivan Illich writes, modernized poverty "combines the lack of power over circumstances with a loss of personal potency"; it is the experience of "frustrating affluence" that occurs in persons "mutilated" by their absolute dependence on industrial productivity. Modernized poverty means enduring life in "an urban landscape that is unfit for people unless they devour each day their own weight in metals, plastics, and fuels, [...] in which the constant need for protection against the unwanted results of more commodities and more commands has generated new depths of discrimination, impotence, and frustration."

Those of us in the global majority find ourselves in a world that tells us that modernized poverty is the best likely outcome for most of us, but that this outcome is only achievable at the cost of exterminating large swathes of living cultures and living nature. At the same time, most of us in the global majority find that we must repress our anger and disgust at the deathly world of suffering we inhabit, if we are to get by and make a decent living for ourselves. What's more, though we may repress our anger and disgust with all our might, most of us find that our anger and disgust inevitably return to the surface, often at the most inopportune moments, often in ways that sabotage our efforts to get by. The most "privileged" amongst us in the global majority are those of us who find ways to decorously express our anger and disgust without overtly threatening or undermining the ruling classes that prevail over, and derive the most pleasures and profits from, this deathly world of suffering. Ay, too many of us "earn" our "privileges" by making it our second nature to redirect our anger and disgust away from the deathly world that oppresses us, and back towards ourselves and/or towards others who are either equally oppressed or even more oppressed.

Having overworked myself these past five years in order to accomplish work that I believe to be meaningful; having had to pay to overwork myself instead of being paid; having struggled to maintain the backhanded privilege of being able to steal time from my employers and squander my paychecks in order to overwork myself; having had to confront the profound horrors of global apartheid and planetary ecocide while overworking myself; having repressed and internalized the profound feelings of anger and disgust provoked by the profound horrors that I confront while overworking myself... All of this is more than enough to explain why I am burning out, and I've still yet to mention the most fundamental and stressful of life's present difficulties: affording ethically and sustainably produced food, clothing, and shelter and endeavoring to care for my loved ones in the midst of economic and ecological crises and a global pandemic.

Putting all of this together makes me wonder... In and through overworking myself these past five years, is it possible that I have been redirecting a portion of my feelings of anger and disgust away from the deathly world that oppresses me and back towards myself?

Indeed, taking a step back and examining my "achievements" over the past five years, I recognize quite clearly that, motivated by feelings of anger and disgust, I have overworked myself in the name of creativity and freedom and, in so doing, yoked my own creativity to the burdensome demands of the white-supremacist capitalist patriarchal cult of productivity. Ay, I recognize and scoff at this ironic situation but, at the same time, I also recognize that I have been stuck between a rock and a hard place.

Inspired by Taoist sages, Zen masters, and contemporary writers like Jenny Odell, I firmly believe that we will never free ourselves from the white-supremacist capitalist patriarchal cult of productivity unless we can effectively learn "how to do nothing." That being said, I also know that few of us today can afford to effectively learn "how to do nothing." Unlike the Taoist sages, Zen masters, and writers like Jenny Odell, I feel that it is necessary to stress the fact that most of us will never effectively learn "how to do nothing" without transforming our world in critical ways. The white-supremacist capitalist patriarchal cult of productivity prevails over most of our world today, and it threatens most of us, especially those of us who are Black, colored, and indigenous, with murder when we are unproductive — disguising so many death threats as matters of routine disciplinary action, as normal(ized) accidents, and as the collateral damage of the pursuit of progressive optimization. Only those of us who have, by ourselves or by proxy, produced more than enough to satisfy the prevailing cult of productivity can afford to learn "how to do nothing" without facing so many disguised death threats.

For the past five years, I have been trying to produce an excess of meaningful creative work in order to satisfy the cult of productivity, hoping that doing so might enable me to afford to learn "how to do nothing" and to help others to do the same. Alas, I have failed in this endeavor, and I am now burning out as a result. I cannot fault myself for failing: without an elite academic degree, without hereditary wealth, and without legacy connections to networks of cultural and social capital, there was only a scant possibility that I would "achieve" my aim. I might fault myself for having devoted an undue amount of my time and energy to reaching for this scant possibility of "achievement" and burning out as a result.

But, then again, what else was I to do? I found myself in a situation not unlike the one described in a curious Zen koan titled, "Incense Regal Stuck High":

Master Incense-Regal Mountain said: "It's like being stuck high in a tree — teeth clamped down on a branch tip, nothing in reach and no footholds anywhere. Someone on the ground calls up, "That ch'i-mind Bodhidharma brought from the West: what is it?"

If you don't answer you deny the question. If you do answer you cut your life short and lose your destiny. Here, now, this moment just like that: how will you answer to save your life?

From Nausicaä of the Valley of the Wind by Hayao Miyazaki

THE
THERA-
PEUTIC
IMAGINA-
TION

I.

There is an essay by John Berger that I love. It is titled "Wanting Now."

I have probably read it two or three dozen times. It is short. It is sweet. It is rousingly life affirming.

That being said, having read it so many times, I have come to be acquainted with places where one might slip in, heave up, and throw out elements of the text in order to shake things up and raise issues to greater attention.

The moment in Berger's essay that I would like to slip into lies in the following passage:

[...] *Not all desires lead to freedom, but freedom is the experience of a desire being acknowledged, chosen and pursued. Desire never concerns the mere possession of something, but the changing of something. Desire is a wanting. A wanting now. Freedom does not constitute the fulfillment of that wanting, but the acknowledgment of its supremacy.*

Berger is rock solid in asserting that "desire never concerns the mere possession of something," but what is meant by the claim that desire concerns "the changing of something?" It is easy for one to (mis)read Berger and argue that he is claiming that it is desire that initiates change, but I believe that Berger is saying something else altogether. It is not that desire initiates change but that desire cares for and nurtures that which is already changing and, in doing so, aims to encourage healthy changes. Desire, then, is a specific kind of wanting; it is a wanting to care or, more simply, desire is a caring. A caring now. Freedom does not constitute the fruition of that caring, but the acknowledgement of its priority.

There is no stopping change: it is not only coming, it is forever ongoing. Individuals and movements cannot initiate changes, nor can they ever stop them; they can only ever relate to change, and they can do so either with or without care. The question is not whether things will change or are changing but, rather, how we might nurture changes in process, and changes we see on the horizon. Those who acknowledge, choose, and pursue their desires are those who relate to change carefully and caringly so as to foster healthy, tonic changes. Those who repress their desires are those who relate to change carelessly and uncaringly, so as to allow unhealthy, toxic changes to take place.

Many of us have been taught to (mis)take desire for its opposite. Those who are desirous, we are taught, will seize every opportunity and grasp whatever they can, destroying much in the process. As long as they get what they want, we are taught, the desirous couldn't care less for the world and its inhabitants. Thus we are taught that desire is a destructive force, and to act on desire is, thus, to negate and destroy.

Nothing could be further from reality than what we are taught.

To negate and destroy is either to restrain, restrict, and repress desire or to lash out against others in reaction to the restraint, restriction, and repression of desire. Blaming frustrated desires for the prevalence of negativity and destructiveness is equivalent to blaming bullied individuals and groups for the prevalence of bullying. It is not the frustrated desire, but the circumstances that frustrate desire, that are to blame for negativity and destructiveness. Again, desire is a caring. It is when people's efforts to take care are frustrated that they become destroyers instead of caretakers. Indeed, the key to making sense of our world today is making sense of the fact that the primary aggressors are not usually the individuals and groups who engage in the spectacular acts of destruction that demand immediate attention. More often than not, the primary aggressors are those who deprive people of any and all motives, means, and opportunities to become caretakers and, instead, furnish them with so many motives, means, and opportunities to become destroyers.

The distinction between desire and cruel destructiveness can be likened to the distinction between power and force.

Power capitalizes on the successful deployment of force. You and I fight, your forces prevail over mine, you win. That is a successful deployment of force, but it is not yet the formation of power. Powers are formed when the winning forces withdraw on the condition that losing forces henceforth comply with their orders. The classic logic in this regard is, "If you don't want to get a whooping like the one that I just delivered to that guy over there, then you'll do what I say when I say it." Rebels are those who disobey power's orders and find out if there truly is a superior force behind a given power.

In a similar fashion, cruel destructiveness capitalizes on the frustrated deployment of desire. You want to care for someone or something, but you are kept from caring. Perhaps to care is to disobey power's orders. Perhaps you are rebuffed by the opposing forces of the other, who has good reason to distrust, or be disgusted by, the ways in which you intend to show care. Whichever the case may be, you react badly to the frustration of your desire and you lash out against the object of your desire. The classic logic in this regard is, "If I can't have you, no one will." But the equivalent logic is, "Knowing that you will not be mine forever, I will use you up while I have you in my grasp." It is a person's childish inability to deal with the frustration of their desire or, more profoundly still, their inability to deal with the prospect that their desire will eventually be frustrated, that leads to cruel destructiveness. The mature person is one who knows how to deal with their frustration without lashing out against the objects of their desire.

The inability to deal with frustrated desire is, as I see it, at the core of patriarchy, and the (con-)fusion of desire with cruel destructiveness defines the patriarchal power formations that prevail over our deathly world of suffering. Take for instance, the perspective of the "Primal Father" in my poem of the same name:

He could not
protect His child
from being taught
difficult lessons
by Mother Nature
but He could beat her
at her own game
by teaching His child
harsh lessons
early and often
before She determined
the time is ripe.

The Primal Father's desire to care for his child is frustrated by Mother Nature, and so the Primal Father becomes cruelly destructive towards his child to spite Mother Nature.

Alternatively, consider the homophobe who violently beats up queer, trans, and gay persons. The homophobe does this because they desire relations with queer, trans, and gay persons but their desires have been frustrated by their fear of being persecuted for desiring queer, trans, and gay persons. This is to say that, in other words, the cruel destructiveness that the homophobe exhibits towards queer, trans, and gay persons is the pathological expression of their frustrated desires for queer, trans, and gay persons. Similarly, the cruel destructiveness that the white-supremacists exhibits towards Black and colored peoples is the pathological expression of their frustrated desires for Black and colored peoples, and the cruel destructiveness of masculinist rape culture towards women is the pathological expression of men's frustrated desires for women. Lacking the maturity to investigate and come to terms with their frustration, the Primal Father, the homophobe, the white-supremacist, and the male chauvinist are all childishly immature: they lash out from frustration, denigrating and destroying the objects of their desires and/or whatever reminds them of such.

II.

The Hollywood imagination would have us believe three things. First, it would have us believe that individuals are responsible for making change and preventing change. Second, it would have us believe that evil are those who actively participate in the most spectacular acts of cruelty and destruction. Third, it would have us believe that unrestrained desire is at the root of all evil.

To this end, the Hollywood imagination works to obscure the fact that evil, in reality, scrupulously insulates itself from spectacular acts of cruelty and destruction and, instead, delights in restraining, restricting, and repressing desire in the subtlest ways, and in depriving people of motives, means, and opportunities to care for themselves and others in the most devious ways. Against the Hollywood imagination, I hold that evil are those who scheme to arrange circumstances to frustrate others' desires in order to cope with the pain of having had their own desires frustrated. Ay, the root of all evil is not desire itself, but the arrangement of circumstances to frustrate desire and encourage spectacular acts of cruelty and destruction thereby.

The evil doer endeavors to destroy the object of their frustrated desire indirectly by frustrating the desire of other persons for the same or similar objects and encouraging them to lash out in destructive ways. The evil doer does not pull the trigger but, instead, grooms triggermen, guarantees them access to guns, and supplies them with ample motives and opportunities to pull the trigger. Though his actions are cruel and destructive, the white male mass shooter who fires upon a crowd of protestors gathered to denounce police brutality is not, himself, evil. Rather, he is the victim and vehicle of evil. Evil are those reactionary politicians and pundits who endeavor to rewrite history and trivialize the horrors of settler-colonialism, white-supremacy, and rape culture; who enable and encourage guns to proliferate; who promote policies to make employment the only way for most people to secure housing, food, and health care, while also pushing policies that increase un/under-employment; who then blame the "woke mob" for the decline of Amerikkkan masculinity and denounce liberal "cucks" and "snowflakes" for taking away good paying jobs from hardworking white men and giving handouts to undeserving women, queers, and Black and colored people.

Going further and digging deeper, the Hollywood imagination would have us believe that heroic figures are those who spectacularly confront those who perpetrate spectacular acts of cruelty and destruction. So-called "anti-fascists" who take their cues from Hollywood movies believe that trading bullets and blows with neo-fascist Proud Boys, Oathkeepers, Boogaloos, police officers and other white triggermen makes them heroes. Again, nothing could be further from reality. Hollywood heroes and their imitators never actually confront evil doers: they only ever confront victims and vehicles of evil. What's more, taking into account the spectacularly cruel and destructive manner in which they confront the victims and vehicles of evil, Hollywood heroes and their imitators are themselves destroyers as opposed to caretakers, which is to say that they are themselves victims and vehicles of evil — lesser victims and vehicles, certainly, but victims and vehicles all the same.

Overstimulating our senses with flashy depictions of the cruel and destructive deeds of greater (villainous) and lesser (heroic) victims and vehicles of evil, the Hollywood imagination displays little regard for desire as caring; little regard for freedom as acknowledging, choosing, and pursuing desire as such; and little regard for countering evil by enabling and enacting freedom as such.

We will not overthrow global apartheid and put a stop to planetary ecocide, the evil scourges of our time, by fighting a war of maneuver against the private and public police, militaries, and paramilitaries who guard de facto and de jure borders and secure the factories, mines, and pipelines that manufacture ecocide. No doubt about it: we will have to defend ourselves against these genocidal, ethnocidal, and ecocidal forces of the evil that are Empire, for they are waging a war against us. However, dedicating all of our energies to waging a heroic war of attrition against these forces in return will be the surest way for us to become and remain victims and vehicles of evil..

If we are to overthrow global apartheid and put a stop to planetary ecocide, we must enable and enact freedom as the acknowledgment, choice, and pursuit of desire as caring, here and now, for changes in process and changes we see on the horizon.

We must be humble in this regard and we mustn't imagine that we can initiate change or put a stop to change. Rather, we must focus and respond to changes happening and likely to happen and do whatever we can do to encourage these changes to develop and unfold in healthy, tonic ways. Sometimes this might mean endeavoring to slow changes, sometimes to speed them up, sometimes to upset their rhythms, sometimes to complement their rhythms. We cannot force changes but we can inflect, deflect, reflect them in tonic ways.

Our inability to force changes is not a flaw but a basic feature of reality that we must leverage against the evil that is Empire. It is Empire, in its hubris, that needs to maintain false claims to have initiated and prevented changes when, in fact, it has only ever inflected, deflected, reflected changes in the most toxic ways.

To think that humans will take the lead in the fight against climate change, for instance, is self-aggrandizing madness. We will need to observe and take our cues from nature, to let forests, shrublands, wetlands, grasslands guide and lead us, rather than forcefully imposing our will on landscapes. The great mistake is to think that all life on Earth, excepting humanity, is mechanically reacting to climate change rather than actively processing and responding to it. We need to carefully observe other lifeforms' diverse responses to climate change in order to carefully and caringly connect and coordinate our own responses with theirs. To recklessly take the lead, disregarding the sensibilities and sensitivities of other lifeforms, is to inflect, deflect, reflect climate changes in toxic ways, furthering planetary ecocide.

Against the Hollywood imagination, the Therapeutic imagination is patiently attentive: it encourages us to take time to attend to what is taking place in order to take careful and caring action with respect to what is taking place. The Therapeutic imagination dispenses with any and all fantasies of heroic good guys swooping in to save the day by beating up bad guys and locking them away. The Therapeutic imagination knows no superheroes but the most under-appreciated healers of the victims and vehicles of evil, those healers who endeavor to "see the spirit of sickness and remove it before it takes shape", as described in the old story with which Thomas Cleary opens his translation of Sun Tzu's Art of War.

A lord of ancient China once asked his physician, a member of a family of healers, which of them was the most skilled in the art.

The physician, whose reputation was such that his name became synonymous with medical science in China, replied, "My eldest brother sees the spirit of sickness and removes it before it takes shape, so his name does not get out of the house.

My elder brother cures illness when it is still extremely minute, so his name does not get out of the neighborhood.

As for me, I puncture veins, prescribe potions, and massage skin, so from time to time my name gets out and is heard among the lords."

Going even further and digging even deeper, the Therapeutic imagination must also be distinguished from the Arthouse imagination. The latter would have us become like nurses who attend scrupulously to the arrangement and sterility of a hospital room, neglecting the patient lying ill in the very same room until the very last second and only in order to snatch them from the throes of death and place them back to teetering on the edge of the abyss. The Arthouse imagination would have us devote our time attending to the place, without ever properly attending to what is taking place, thereby keeping us from ever taking careful and caring action with respect to what is taking place. In other words, the Arthouse imagination would have us scrupulously attend to forms while neglecting their contents.

By contrast, with profound sensitivity and subtlety, the Therapeutic imagination stays with the trouble of continuously varying forms, faulting and repairing them in order to better convey and care for their ever changing contents. This process of staying with the trouble is a rhythmic process in which moments of patient attention (during which forms are subjected to stresses and strains as their contents change) are syncopated with moments of careful and caring action (during which forms are repaired and rested in order to better convey and care for their changed and changing contents).

The Therapeutic imagination's syncopation of moments of patient attention, on the one hand, and careful and caring action, on the other, should be contrasted with the Hollywood imagination's chain reactions, in which action alternates with reaction to create a domino effect, each successive action being a reaction to the preceding action. The chain reactions of the Hollywood imagination narrativize the back and forth between greater (villainous) and lesser (heroic) victims and vehicles of evil without properly recognizing evil doers and evil deeds.

The rhythms of the Therapeutic imagination should also be contrasted with those of the Arthouse imagination, which syncopates moments of orchestration, during which the dominoes are set up, with chain reactions, during which the dominoes fall. By featuring moments of orchestration, the Arthouse imagination recognizes the evil deed and the evil doer but, lacking moments of patient attention and moments of careful and caring action, the Arthouse imagination does not properly recognize healers and healing processes.

Only the Therapeutic imagination recognizes healers and healing processes by and through its syncopation of moments of patient attention and moments of careful and caring action.

In every life, there will be periods during which the Arthouse imagination appeals to and prevails over us, periods during which the Hollywood imagination appeals and prevails, and periods during which the Therapeutic imagination appeals and prevails. It is impossible to lead a life that knows nothing of the appeal of the Hollywood and Arthouse imaginations, but we can and must do everything one can to maximize the appeal and the prevalence of the Therapeutic imagination, and minimize that of the Hollywood and Arthouse imaginations. This is how we will learn to recognize those deserting the forces of Empire and defecting to the forces of Nature.

AGAINST GLOBAL APARTHEID & PLANETARY ECOCIDE

A.G.A.P.E.

Imagine a world in which political geographies are drawn by the ever changing flows of freshwater that are vital to life on Earth, so that all borders become fluid and dynamic; a world in which territorial nations are abolished, so that all nations become, in effect, diasporic nations; a world in which each and every geopolitical unit is a fluid multi-national body inclusive of all the different diasporas that suffuse a given freshwater ecoregion; a world in which the many multitudes of the diffuse diasporas and all of the different ecoregional bodies are included within a planetary body that makes plans pertaining to the freshwaters of the ecosphere as a whole.

We, the anti-colonial ecoregionalists of the 21st century — the wild and unruly bastards of the 20th century's anti-colonial nationalists, the land defenders and the water protectors — are endeavoring to make this world a reality.

In striving to realize this world, we are struggling against the various forms of inter-national and intra-national colonialism presently administering the cruel pleasures and foul profits of genocide, ethnocide, and ecocide according to the racist logic of global apartheid; and we are struggling for the nurture and care of the beautiful and differentiated languages, cultures, customs, and ways of life of the Earth's people, which are vital to the health of the planet.

Our world-making project turns on four spokes.

FREE MIGRATION & THE DIASPORIZATION OF NATIONAL IDENTITIES.

Against territorial nationalism. — Free migration and the diasporization of national identities does not imply the obliteration of nations' roots but, rather, the creeping of their roots and the spreading of their branches and leaves. For instance, the roots of the Black African diaspora remain deep in Sub-Saharan Africa but they have crept outward into the Caribbean Islands and the Americas and, what's more, branches and leaves of the African diaspora can now be found all over the globe.

THE CREOLIZATION OF ETHNIC & RACIAL IDENTITIES.

Against Eurocentrism, white supremacy, anti-blackness, and all other forms of ethnocentrism and racism. — The creolization of ethnic and racial identities does not imply the obliteration of races and ethnicities but, rather, their continuous variation. The writings of Édouard Glissant tell of how the creolization of the peoples of the Black Atlantic has not produced a fixed monolithic monoculture but, instead, many improvised polyrhythmic polycultures. Creolization is not the homogenizing assimilation of the many into one (*"e pluribus unum"*) but the hybridizing proliferation of the many into more (*"e pluribus multis"*).

THE QUEERING OF GENDER & SEXUAL IDENTITIES.

Against patriarchal sexism. — Similar to the creolization of ethnic and racial identities, the queering of gender and sexual identities does not imply the obliteration of genders and sexes but, rather, their continuous variation. The queering of gender and sexual identities neither yields a single gray gender identity nor a single gray sexual orientation but, instead, yields colorful spectra of transitional and transitory genders and polymorphously perverse sexualities.

Given that different cultures configure their gender and sexual identities differently, the queering of gender and sexual identities is, in fact, coterminous with the creolization of ethnic and racial identities. That being said, we must separately emphasize the queering of gender and sexual identities because the hetero-patriarchal power formations that prevail over our world today are particularly hostile towards the queering of gender and sexual identities that follows from the creolization of ethnic and racial identities.

CONVIVIAL COMMUNISM.

Against industrial capitalism. — Convivial communism does not imply the obliteration of industrial capitalism but, rather, its marginalization. Convivial communism centers relations of production that provide for social subsistence, and it marginalizes relations of production that impede social subsistence.

Industrial capitalism, by contrast, centers relations of production that privilege capital accumulation, and it marginalizes relations of production that impede capital accumulation, with an extreme prejudice against the relations of production that deep rooting indigenous peoples have developed to provide for social subsistence.

Whereas industrial capitalism endeavors to liquidate any and all relations of subsistence that are determined to be unprofitable, convivial communism endeavors to enable wildly different relations of subsistence to proliferate and radiate mutualistically, together in Relation, regardless of their profitability.

The maneuvers with which we steer the wheels of our world-making project are three.

TAKING DIRECT ACTION

Against rights activism and against protest as an appeal to authority — we defy any and all forms of stable, non-consensual, and non-negotiable authority.

As David Graeber once put it, the difference between protest and direct action is that protest, however militant, is an appeal to authorities to behave differently; by contrast, direct action is a matter of proceeding as one would if the existing structure of power did not exist or, to be more precise, as if the existing structure of power is unstable and consensually (re-)negotiable as opposed to stable, non-consensual, and non-negotiable.

Our motto: *Better to defy authority than appeal to it.*

MAKING CASES.

Against legislating rules and regulations — we defend direct actions with due process.

As Gilles Deleuze once put it, all of the abominations through which humans have suffered are cases: not denials of abstract rights, but abominable cases. One can say that these cases resemble each other, have something in common, but that only makes them situations for jurisprudence and due process, not for the abstract legislation of rights. For us, politics is a matter of inventing jurisprudences and forms of due process such that, following each abominable case, plans are made to ward off and protect against the recurrence of the same and similar such abominations.

Our motto: *Never legislate when you can litigate.*

MAKING PLANS

Against formulating policies and charging police officers with securing compliance with said policies — we establish planning bodies and charge planners with negotiating dissensus and finding consensus, so that all who are involved and affected by a given plan recognize their needs and feelings in the given plan.

As Fred Moten and Stefano Harney once put it, planning is a means to develop supportive and sustainable communities along with others. Policy, by contrast, is means to administer scarcity and precarity for the sake of others and on behalf of others.

Our motto: *Don't make policy for others, make plans with them.*

OUTRO:
REVOLUTIONARY
LOVE
(FOR JOY JAMES)

Slave masters, capitalists, and colonizers are parasitic beings. They sustain and pleasure themselves by extracting from and destroying the bodies, the minds, the spirits, and the lands of the captive peoples whom they violently (re-)make into chattel slaves, wage slaves, and colonized subjects.

Slave masters, capitalists, and colonizers have managed to sustain and pleasure themselves in this way for centuries by ensuring the minimum social reproduction of their victims: exploiting their victims' capacities to give birth, to love, and to care for one another despite suffering the exploitative indignities of dispossession, denigration, and deprivation.

Captive lovers and captive maternals are those chattel slaves, wage slaves, and colonized subjects whose capacity for (re-)birth and for loving and caring are exploited to effectively ensure the social reproduction of ever more chattel slaves, wage slaves, and colonized subjects. Captive lovers and captive maternals provide the minimal love and care that is socially necessary to enable their fellow victims of slavery and colonization to endure their exploitation without starving, succumbing to illness, burning out, losing their minds, committing suicide, or self-destructively lashing out against their oppressors. Our captive lovers and captive maternals enable us to sleep, to wake up, and to labor, day after day, even when all we can expect from every next day is the continuation of our oppression.

The Hollywood Imagination often celebrates captive love and captive maternity. It celebrates the romantic couple that endures exploitative indignities, overcoming the odds stacked against them in order to "stay together" in an unjust and unequal world. It celebrates the parents who suffer dispossession, denigration, and deprivation but take solace in the fact that they are "doing it for the kids," that their hard work will give their kids a shot at making the cut and joining the "talented tenth" that is spared the indignities of dispossession, denigration, and deprivation. It celebrates the nurses and social workers who care for the most abject victims of colonization and slavery, helping unfortunates back on their feet and holding their hands so that the injustices and inequities that continue to batter them do not knock them flat on their backs again. These and other similarly tragic figures are often sainted as "redeemers" by the Hollywood Imagination, which aims to convince us that the root of our suffering is not our captivity but our being unloved and uncared for in our captivity and as captives.

In the real world, captive love and captive maternity are misfortunes that we are compelled to give and receive from one another. Giving and receiving them requires that we repress our awareness of disturbing realities, covering up the facts of racial capitalist genocides, ethnocides, and ecocides with so many wishful and defensive fantasies. Our repressed awareness of these disturbing realities inevitably stirs up feelings of frustration and resentment in us, and captive love and captive maternity quickly turn into hate and cruelty, often directed at "others" whom we make scapegoats for the frustrations and resentments engendered by captive love and captive maternity.

Healthy forms of love and care cannot exist under captivity; they can only emerge in and through the process of refusing, resisting, and escaping captivity in pursuit of autonomy.

Revolutionary lovers and maternals are those who refuse to acquiesce to captivity and, instead, love and nurture their kin in ways that undermine the forces and power formations that make people into chattel slaves, wage slaves, and colonized subjects.

Only those who give and receive revolutionary love and care are able to self-actualize in healthy, tonic ways by refusing, resisting, and escaping the indignities of dispossession, denigration, and deprivation. Otherwise, without giving and receiving revolutionary love and care, one's own self-actualization will be toxic, as it can only be achieved at the expense of a captive lover or captive maternal.

The Hollywood Imagination often presents us with a false dichotomy: either assume the role of captive lover and captive maternal, or abandon your kin in order to "join the revolution," "find your higher calling," etc. The Hollywood Imagination cannot properly recognize that the revolutionary does not self-actualize by abandoning their kin but, rather, loves and cares for their kin by enabling their kin to gather the community, the intellectual and material resources, and the spirit required to refuse, resist, and escape captivity in pursuit of autonomy. It is the revolutionary who is abandoned by their kin when their kin only seek to give and receive captive love and care and reject the giving and receiving of revolutionary love and care.

The Therapeutic Imagination counters the false dichotomies and the wishful and defensive fantasies that are typical of the Hollywood Imagination. The Therapeutic Imagination refuses to romanticize captive love and captive maternity and, instead, exposes how oppressors exploit captive love and captive maternity in order to reproduce victims of oppression. What's more, going further, the Therapeutic Imagination helps us make sense of what it takes to be a revolutionary lover and caregiver. It teaches us to dispense with the notion that love enables us to overcome adversity and "make it" in a toxic world, and they teach us to embrace the notion that love is the labor of helping each other to refuse, resist, and escape a toxic world and contribute to the (re-)creation of a tonic world.

We are accomplices of slave masters, capitalists, and colonizers and enablers of the fetishes of Empire insofar as we embrace the role of captive lover and captive maternal and succumb to the wishful and defensive fantasies pushed by the Hollywood Imagination, insofar as we convince ourselves that we can "make it" in a toxic world and leave the hard work of (re-)creating a tonic world to others.

Why do we remain so deeply attached to forms of love that are premised on racial, colonial, and ecological violence, and that presume and project the prevalence of so much violence out into the future? What personal and ancestral traumas bind us to the forces of Empire? Are we conditioned to fear being abandoned by those who will only ever accept us as captive lovers and maternals? Or, to be more precise, is it that we are too afraid to admit to ourselves that, by giving and receiving of captive love and captive maternity, we have already been abandoned, both by our loved ones and ourselves?

We desert the forces of Empire and defect to the forces of Nature when we challenge ourselves to give and receive revolutionary love and, in the same gesture, challenge our loved ones to receive and give revolutionary love in return. In so doing, we also confront our fear of being abandoned and the processes of traumatization that have instilled this fear in us. But in challenging ourselves and our loved ones to give and receive revolutionary love, we do not risk abandonment, but recognize abandonment for what it is and, what's more, free ourselves to divest our time and energy from relations predicated upon our abandonment and to invest in mutual relations of revolutionary love with those who desire.

No one can refuse, resist, and escape today's toxic world and (re-)create a tonic world for themselves alone, without giving and receiving revolutionary love. The extension of revolutionary love to others, human and non-human, living and dead, has been and will continue to be both the beginning and the end of all truly radical peoples movements. These movements are not defined by the powers and privileges that they seize from the ruling classes and for themselves but, rather, by everyday acts of revolutionary love that condition and enable people to exercise their fundamental freedoms — to flee, to rebel, to (de-/re-)construct worlds — without fear of abandonment and punishment.

From Nausicaä of the Valley of the Wind by Hayao Miyazaki

Milton Keynes UK
Ingram Content Group UK Ltd.
UKHW051941240823
427328UK00004B/63